Microsoft
PowerPoint 2002

Introductory Concepts and Techniques

Gary B. Shelly
Thomas J. Cashman
Susan L. Sebok

COURSE
TECHNOLOGY
THOMSON LEARNING

COURSE TECHNOLOGY
25 THOMSON PLACE
BOSTON MA 02210

SHELLY
CASHMAN
SERIES®

Australia • Canada • Denmark • Japan • Mexico • New Zealand • Philippines • Puerto Rico • Singapore
South Africa • Spain • United Kingdom • United States

COURSE TECHNOLOGY

THOMSON LEARNING

COPYRIGHT © 2002 Course Technology, a division of Thomson Learning.
Printed in the United States of America

Asia (excluding Japan)
Thomson Learning
60 Albert Street, #15-01
Albert Complex
Singapore 189969

Japan
Thomson Learning
Palaceside Building 5F
1-1-1 Hitotsubashi, Chiyoda-ku
Tokyo 100 0003 Japan

Australia/New Zealand
Nelson/Thomson Learning
102 Dodds Street
South Melbourne, Victoria 3205
Australia

Latin America
Thomson Learning
Seneca, 53
Colonia Polanco
11560 Mexico D.F. Mexico

South Africa
Thomson Learning
Zonnebloem Building,
Constantia Square
526 Sixteenth Road
P.O. Box 2459
Halfway House, 1685
South Africa

Canada
Nelson/Thomson Learning
1120 Birchmount Road
Scarborough, Ontario
Canada M1K 5G4

UK/Europe/Middle East
Thomson Learning
Berkshire House
168-173 High Holborn
London, WC1V 7AA United Kingdom

Spain
Thomson Learning
Calle Magallanes, 25
28015-MADRID
ESPANA

PHOTO CREDITS: *Microsoft PowerPoint 2002 Project 1, pages PP 1.04-05* Business people, cell phone, circuit boards and gears, fiber optic cable, notebook computer, number printout, telephone jack, utility wires and towers, world on computer screen, Courtesy of PhotoDisc, Inc.; *Project 2, pages PP 2.02-03* Conference room meeting, office meeting, three businesspeople, woman in taxi, woman speaking at a meeting, Courtesy of PhotoDisc, Inc.

ISBN 0-7895-6283-9

2 3 4 5 6 7 8 9 10   BC   06 05 04 03 02

Microsoft
PowerPoint 2002
Introductory Concepts and Techniques

Contents

Preface

The Shelly Cashman Series® offers the finest textbooks in computer education. We are proud of the fact that our series of Microsoft Office 4.3, Microsoft Office 95, Microsoft Office 97, and Microsoft Office 2000 textbooks have been the most widely used books in education. With each new edition of our Office books, we have made improvements based on the software and comments made by the instructors and students. The *Microsoft Office XP* books continue with the innovation, quality, and reliability that you have come to expect from the Shelly Cashman Series.

In this *Microsoft PowerPoint 2002* book, you will find an educationally sound and easy-to-follow pedagogy that combines a step-by-step approach with corresponding screens. All projects and exercises in this book are designed to take full advantage of the PowerPoint 2002 enhancements. The popular Other Ways and More About features offer in-depth knowledge of PowerPoint 2002. The new Learn It Online page presents a wealth of additional exercises to ensure your students have all the reinforcement they need. The project openers provide a fascinating perspective of the subject covered in the project. The project material is developed carefully to ensure that students will see the importance of learning PowerPoint for future coursework.

Objectives of This Textbook

Microsoft PowerPoint 2002: Introductory Concepts and Techniques is intended for a course that covers a brief introduction to PowerPoint 2002. No experience with a computer is assumed, and no mathematics beyond the high school freshman level is required. The objectives of this book are:

- ■ To teach the fundamentals of PowerPoint 2002
- ■ To expose students to practical examples of the computer as a useful tool
- ■ To acquaint students with the proper procedures to create presentations
- ■ To develop an exercise-oriented approach that allows learning by doing
- ■ To introduce students to new input technologies
- ■ To encourage independent study, and help those who are working alone

The Shelly Cashman Approach

Features of the Shelly Cashman Series *Microsoft PowerPoint 2002* books include:

- ■ **Project Orientation:** Each project in the book presents a practical problem and complete solution in an easy-to-understand approach.
- ■ **Step-by-Step, Screen-by-Screen Instructions:** Each of the tasks required to complete a project is identified throughout the project. Full-color screens accompany the steps.
- ■ **Thoroughly Tested Projects:** Every screen in the book is correct because it is produced by the author only after performing a step, resulting in unprecedented quality.
- ■ **Other Ways Boxes and Quick Reference Summary:** The Other Ways boxes displayed at the end of most of the step-by-step sequences specify the other ways to do the task completed in the steps. Thus, the steps and the Other Ways box make a comprehensive reference unit.
- ■ **More About Feature:** These marginal annotations provide background information and tips that complement the topics covered, adding depth and perspective.

Other **Ways**

1. On Insert menu click New Slide
2. Press CTRL+M
3. In Voice Command mode, say "New Slide"

More *About*

Slide Space

Some blank space on a slide can be advantageous. The absence of text, called white space, helps the viewer focus attention on the presenter. Do not be afraid to leave some white space on your slide to give your text and visual elements some breathing room.

v

■ Integration of the World Wide Web: The World Wide Web is integrated into the PowerPoint 2002 learning experience by (1) More About annotations that send students to Web sites for up-to-date information and alternative approaches to tasks; (2) a MOUS information Web page so students can prepare for the MOUS Certification examinations; (3) an PowerPoint 2002 Quick Reference Summary Web page that summarizes the ways to complete tasks (mouse, menu, shortcut menu, and keyboard); and (4) the Learn It Online page at the end of each project, which has project reinforcement exercises, learning games, and other types of student activities.

Organization of This Textbook

Microsoft PowerPoint 2002: Introductory Concepts and Techniques provides basic instruction on how to use PowerPoint 2002. The material is divided into two projects, a Web Feature, five appendices, and a Quick Reference Summary.

Project 1 – Using a Design Template and Text Slide Layout to Create a Presentation In Project 1, students are introduced to PowerPoint terminology, the PowerPoint window, and the basics of creating a bulleted list presentation.

Project 2 – Using the Outline Tab and Clip Art to Create a Slide Show In Project 2, students create a presentation from an outline, insert clip art, and add animation effects.

Web Feature – Creating a Presentation on the Web Using PowerPoint In the Web Feature, students are introduced to saving a presentation as a Web page.

Appendices The book includes five appendices. Appendix A presents an introduction to the Microsoft PowerPoint Help system. Appendix B describes how to use the speech and handwriting recognition capabilities of PowerPoint 2002. Appendix C explains how to publish Web pages to a Web server. Appendix D shows how to reset the menus and toolbars. Appendix E introduces students to the Microsoft Office User Specialist (MOUS) Certification program.

Quick Reference Summary In Microsoft PowerPoint 2002, you can accomplish a task in a number of ways, such as using the mouse, menu, shortcut menu, and keyboard. The Quick Reference Summary at the back of the book provides a quick reference to each task presented.

End-of-Project Student Activities

A notable strength of the Shelly Cashman Series *Microsoft PowerPoint 2002* books is the extensive student activities at the end of each project. Well-structured student activities can make the difference between students merely participating in a class and students retaining the information they learn. The activities in the Shelly Cashman Series *PowerPoint 2002* books include the following.

■ **What You Should Know** A listing of the tasks completed within a project together with the pages on which the step-by-step, screen-by-screen explanations appear.

■ **Learn It Online** Every project features a Learn It Online page comprised of ten exercises. These exercises include True/False, Multiple Choice, Short Answer, Flash Cards, Practice Test, Learning Games, Tips and Tricks, Newsgroup usage, Expanding Your Horizons, and Search Sleuth.

■ **Apply Your Knowledge** This exercise usually requires students to open and manipulate a file on the Data Disk. To obtain a copy of the Data Disk, follow the instructions on the inside back cover of this textbook.

- **In the Lab** Three in-depth assignments per project require students to apply the knowledge gained in the project to solve problems on a computer.
- **Cases and Places** Up to seven unique real-world case-study situations.

Shelly Cashman Series Teaching Tools

The three basic ancillaries that accompany this textbook are: Teaching Tools (ISBN 0-7895-6323-1), Course Presenter (ISBN 0-7895-6466-1), and MyCourse.com. These ancillaries are available to adopters through your Course Technology representative or by calling one of the following telephone numbers: Colleges and Universities, 1-800-648-7450; High Schools, 1-800-824-5179; Private Career Colleges, 1-800-477-3692; Canada, 1-800-268-2222; and Corporations and Government Agencies, 1-800-340-7450.

Teaching Tools

The contents of the Teaching Tools CD-ROM are listed below.

- **Instructor's Manual** The Instructor's Manual includes the following for each project: project objectives; project overview; detailed lesson plans with page number references; teacher notes and activities; answers to the end-of-project exercises; a test bank of 110 questions for every project (25 multiple-choice, 50 true/false, and 35 fill-in-the-blank) with page number references; and transparency references. The transparencies are available through the Figures in the Book. The test bank questions are the same as in ExamView and Course Test Manager.
- **Figures in the Book** Illustrations for every screen and table in the textbook are available in electronic form. Use this ancillary to present a slide show in lecture or to print transparencies for use in lecture with an overhead projector.
- **ExamView** ExamView is a state-of-the-art test builder that is easy to use. With ExamView, you quickly can create printed tests, Internet tests, and computer (LAN-based) tests. You can enter your own test questions or use the test bank that accompanies ExamView. The test bank is the same as the one described in the Instructor's Manual section. Instructors who want to continue to use our earlier generation test builder, Course Test Manager, rather than ExamView, can call Customer Service at 1-800-648-7450 for a copy of the Course Test Manager database for this book.
- **Course Syllabus** Any instructor who has been assigned a course at the last minute knows how difficult it is to come up with a course syllabus. For this reason, sample syllabi are included that can be customized easily to a course.
- **Lecture Success System** Lecture Success System files are used to explain and illustrate the step-by-step, screen-by-screen development of a project in the textbook without entering large amounts of data.
- **Instructor's Lab Solutions** Solutions and required files for all the In the Lab assignments at the end of each project are available. Solutions also are available for any Cases and Places assignment that supplies data.
- **Lab Tests/Test Outs** Tests that parallel the In the Lab assignments are supplied for the purpose of testing students in the laboratory on the material covered in the project or testing students out of the course.
- **Project Reinforcement** True/false, multiple choice, and short answer questions.
- **Student Files** All the files that are required by students to complete the Apply Your Knowledge exercises are included.
- **Interactive Labs** Eighteen completely updated, hands-on Interactive Labs that take students from ten to fifteen minutes each to step through help solidify and reinforce mouse and keyboard usage and computer concepts. Student assessment is available.

Course Presenter

Course Presenter is a lecture presentation system that provides PowerPoint slides for each project. Presentations are based on the projects' objectives. Use this presentation system to present well-organized lectures that are both interesting and knowledge-based. Course Presenter provides consistent coverage at schools that use multiple lecturers in their applications courses.

MyCourse.com

MyCourse.com offers instructors and students an opportunity to supplement classroom learning with additional course content. You can use mycourse.com to expand on traditional learning by completing readings, tests, and other assignments through the customized, comprehensive Web site. For additional information, visit mycourse.com and click the Help button.

SAM XP

SAM XP is a powerful skills-based testing and reporting tool that measures your students' proficiency in Microsoft Office applications through real-world, performance-based questions. SAM XP is available for a minimal cost.

Acknowledgments

The Shelly Cashman Series would not be the leading computer education series without the contributions of outstanding publishing professionals. First, and foremost, among them is Becky Herrington, director of production and designer. She is the heart and soul of the Shelly Cashman Series, and it is only through her leadership, dedication, and tireless efforts that superior products are made possible.

Under Becky's direction, the following individuals made significant contributions to these books: Doug Cowley, production manager; Ginny Harvey, series specialist and developmental editor; Ken Russo, senior Web and graphic designer; Mike Bodnar, associate production manager; Mark Norton, Web designer; Betty Hopkins and Richard Herrera, interior design; Meena Moest, product review manager, Bruce Greene, multimedia product manager; Michelle French, Christy Otten, Stephanie Nance, Chris Schneider, Sharon Lee Nelson, Sarah Boger, Amanda Lotter, and Michael Greko, graphic artists; Jeanne Black and Betty Hopkins, Quark experts; Lyn Markowicz, Nancy Lamm, Kim Kosmatka, Pam Baxter, and Marilyn Martin, copyeditors/proofreaders; Cristina Haley, proofreader/indexer; Sarah Evertson of Image Quest, photo researcher; Ginny Harvey, Rich Hansberger, Kim Clark, and Nancy Smith, contributing writers; and Richard Herrera, cover design.

Finally, we would like to thank Richard Keaveny, associate publisher; John Sisson, managing editor; Jim Quasney, series consulting editor; Erin Roberts, product manager; Erin Runyon, associate product manager; Francis Schurgot and Marc Ouellette, Web product managers; Rachel VanKirk, marketing manager; and Reed Cotter, editorial assistant.

Gary B. Shelly
Thomas J. Cashman
Susan L. Sebok

Microsoft PowerPoint 2002

Using a Design Template and Text Slide Layout to Create a Presentation

You will have mastered the material in this project when you can:

- Start and customize PowerPoint
- Describe the PowerPoint window
- Describe the speech recognition capabilities of PowerPoint
- Select a design template
- Create a title slide
- Change the font size and font style
- Save a presentation
- Add a new slide
- Create a text slide with a single-level bulleted list
- Create a text slide with a multi-level bulleted list
- End a slide show with a black slide
- Move to another slide in normal view
- View a presentation in slide show view
- Quit PowerPoint
- Open a presentation
- Check spelling and consistency, correct errors, and edit a presentation
- Display a presentation in black and white
- Print a presentation in black and white
- Use the PowerPoint Help system to answer your questions

COMDEX Glitz

Presentations Dazzle the Masses

Thousands of the world's computer industry executives attend, including keynote speakers, Bill Gates, Andy Grove, and Michael Dell. They are joined by hundreds of thousands of technology enthusiasts, industry professionals, and curious spectators seeking the latest trends in hardware, software, and the Internet, as well as the hottest new gizmos, gadgets, and games.

They will be attending COMDEX, North America's largest trade show. COMDEX/Fall is held in Las Vegas each November, and COMDEX/Spring is held in Chicago in April. Both shows feature speeches by industry leaders, tutorials on the latest technologies, and thousands of square feet of exhibits showcasing the latest in computer technology.

Information technology (IT) experts headline COMDEX as the premier IT event in the world. Indeed, more than 10,000 new products are unveiled at the Fall show. Since COMDEX's inception in 1979, some of the more notable product launches have been the IBM PC in 1981, COMPAQ's suitcase-sized portable computer, Microsoft's first version of Windows, Apple's original Macintosh computer, and CD-ROM drives, and the promise of wireless technology utilizing the Bluetooth™ standard.

Attendance and industry representation have grown steadily. The first show featured 150 exhibitions seen by 4,000 curious visitors. Six years later, more than 1,000 companies displayed their wares for more than 100,000 techies. Recent shows have produced as many as 2,400 booths visited by 250,000-plus attendees.

Computer companies realize their sales forces need to capture their audiences' attention, so they add sensory cues to their exhibits. They treat the trade show visitors to a multimedia blitz of sound, visuals, and action with the help of presentation software such as Microsoft PowerPoint 2002. This program enhances the presenters' speeches by highlighting keywords in the presentation, displaying graphs, pictures, and diagrams, and playing sound and video clips.

In this project, you will learn to use PowerPoint 2002 to create a presentation (also called a slide show) for a Westview College counselors' orientation using a design template and one of PowerPoint's layouts. Then, you will run the slide show and print audience handouts.

PowerPoint's roots stem from the innovative work performed by a small company called Forethought, Inc. Programmers at this pioneering business coined the phrase, desktop presentation graphics, for formal slide shows and created a complete software package that automated creating slides containing text, charts, and graphics. Microsoft liked the visual appeal of the software and acquired Forethought in 1987. Company executives decided to market the software to Apple Macintosh users because Mac computers were considered clearly superior to IBM-based personal computers for graphics applications.

Microsoft PowerPoint became a favorite among Mac users. Meanwhile, Lotus Freelance Graphics and Software Publishing Harvard Graphics were popular within the PC community. This division ceased, however, when Microsoft released Windows 3.0 in 1990 and subsequently developed a Windows version of PowerPoint to run on PCs.

Since that time, Macintosh and PC users alike have utilized the presentation power of PowerPoint. The package has grown to include animation, audio and video clips, and Internet integration. Certainly the technology gurus at COMDEX have realized PowerPoint's dazzling visual appeal. So will you as you complete the exercises in this textbook.

Microsoft PowerPoint 2002

Using a Design Template and Text Slide Layout to Create a Presentation

PROJECT

CASE PERSPECTIVE

As a receptionist in your college's counseling office, you meet students who are waiting for their scheduled appointments. You have noticed that many of them seem sad. They sit silently and do not make eye contact or speak with their fellow students.

Because of your concern, you mention this observation to Jennifer Williams, the dean of counseling. She tells you that most college students are lonely. In fact, a Carnegie study finds that only 36 percent of college students participate in student activities other than sports. Consequently, they are self-absorbed and miss the joys of college. She says that Intro to Loneliness would be one class that would fill quickly because loneliness is one of college students' worst enemies. Many of these students do not adjust well to the initial move from home, which makes it difficult for them to meet new people and make friends. Therefore, they play it safe and stay by themselves.

You suggest that counselors discuss this loneliness at freshmen orientation, and Jennifer agrees. She knows you are proficient at PowerPoint and asks you to develop a presentation focusing on how to make friends on campus.

What Is Microsoft PowerPoint?

Microsoft PowerPoint is a complete presentation graphics program that allows you to produce professional looking presentations. A PowerPoint **presentation** also is called a **slide show**. PowerPoint gives you the flexibility to make presentations using a projection device attached to a personal computer (Figure 1-1a) and using overhead transparencies (Figure 1-1b). In addition, you can take advantage of the World Wide Web and run virtual presentations on the Internet (Figure 1-1c). PowerPoint also can create paper printouts of the individual slides, outlines, and speaker notes.

PowerPoint contains several features to simplify creating a slide show. For example, you can instruct PowerPoint to create a predesigned presentation, and then you can modify the presentation to fulfill your requirements. You quickly can format a slide show using one of the professionally designed presentation design templates. To make your presentation more impressive, you can add tables, charts, pictures, video, sound, and animation effects. You also can check the spelling or style of your slide show as you type or after you have completed designing the presentation. For example, you can instruct PowerPoint to restrict the number of bulleted items on a slide or limit the number of words in each paragraph. Additional PowerPoint features include the following:

- **Word processing** — create bulleted lists, combine words and images, find and replace text, and use multiple fonts and type sizes.
- **Outlining** — develop your presentation using an outline format. You also can import outlines from Microsoft Word or other word processing programs.
- **Charting** — create and insert charts into your presentations. The two chart types are: standard, which includes bar, line, pie, and xy (scatter) charts; and custom, which displays such objects as floating bars, colored lines, and three-dimensional cones.

(a) Projection Device Connected to a Personal Computer

(b) Overhead Transparencies

(c) PowerPoint Presentation on the World Wide Web

FIGURE 1-1

Microsoft **PowerPoint 2002**

Microportable Projectors

Light, sleek multimedia projectors are extremely popular. The newer devices weigh less than three pounds and can be held in one hand. They offer zooms, contrast controls, and HDTV support. For more information, visit the PowerPoint 2002 More About Web page (scsite.com/pp2002/more.htm) and then click Projectors.

▶ **Drawing** — form and modify diagrams using shapes such as arcs, arrows, cubes, rectangles, stars, and triangles.

▶ **Inserting multimedia** — insert artwork and multimedia effects into your slide show. The Microsoft Media Gallery contains hundreds of clip art images, pictures, photos, sounds, and video clips. You can search for clips by entering words or phrases that describe the subject you want by looking for clips with similar artistic styles, colors, or shapes, or by connecting to a special Web site just for clip art. You also can import art from other applications.

▶ **Web support** — save presentations or parts of a presentation in HTML format so they can be viewed and manipulated using a browser. You can publish your slide show to the Internet or to an intranet. You also can insert action buttons and hyperlinks to create a self-running or interactive Web presentation.

▶ **E-mailing** — send your entire slide show as an attachment to an e-mail message.

▶ **Using Wizards** — create a presentation quickly and efficiently by answering prompts for specific content criteria. For example, the **AutoContent Wizard** gives prompts for the type of slide show you are planning, such as communicating serious news or motivating a team, and the type of output, such as an on-screen presentation or black and white overheads. If you are planning to run your presentation on another computer, the **Pack and Go Wizard** helps you bundle everything you need, including any objects associated with that presentation. If you cannot confirm that this other computer has PowerPoint installed, you also can include the **PowerPoint Viewer**, a program that allows you to run, but not edit, a PowerPoint slide show.

Project One — Time to Start Making Friends

PowerPoint allows you to produce slides similar to those you would develop in an academic or business environment. In Project 1, you create the presentation shown in Figures 1-2a through 1-2d. The objective is to produce a presentation, called Time to Start Making Friends, to display using a projection device. As an introduction to PowerPoint, this project steps you through the most common type of presentation, which is a **text slide** consisting of a bulleted list. A **bulleted list** is a list of paragraphs, each preceded by a bullet. A **bullet** is a symbol such as a heavy dot (•) or other character that precedes text when the text warrants special emphasis.

(a) Slide 1

(b) Slide 2

(c) Slide 3

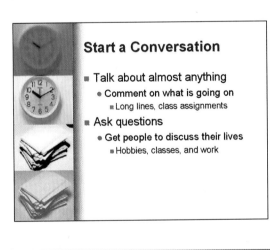

(d) Slide 4

FIGURE 1-2

Starting and Customizing PowerPoint

To start PowerPoint, Windows must be running. The quickest way to begin a new presentation is to use the **Start button** on the **Windows taskbar** at the bottom of the screen. Perform these steps to start PowerPoint and a new presentation, or ask your instructor how to start PowerPoint for your system.

Steps To Start PowerPoint

1 **Click the Start button on the Windows taskbar, point to Programs on the Start menu, and then point to Microsoft PowerPoint on the Programs submenu.**

The commands on the Start menu display above the Start button and the Programs submenu displays (Figure 1-3). If the Office Speech Recognition software is installed on your computer, then the Language bar may display somewhere on the desktop.

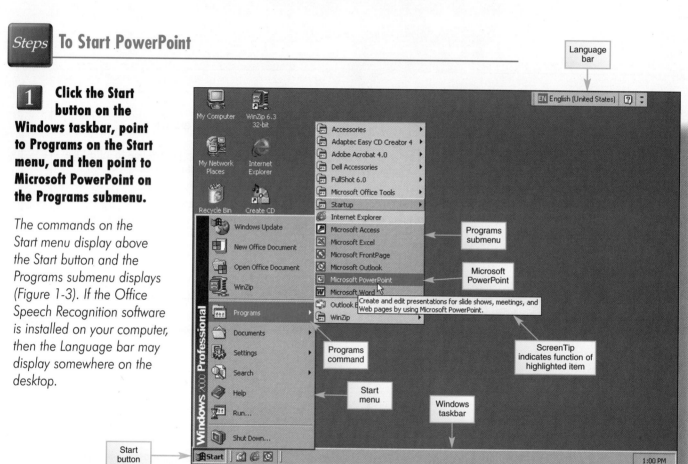

FIGURE 1-3

2 **Click PowerPoint.**

PowerPoint starts. While PowerPoint is starting, the mouse pointer changes to the shape of an hourglass. After a few moments, a blank presentation titled Presentation1 displays in the PowerPoint window (Figure 1-4).

3 **If the PowerPoint window is not maximized, double-click its title bar to maximize it.**

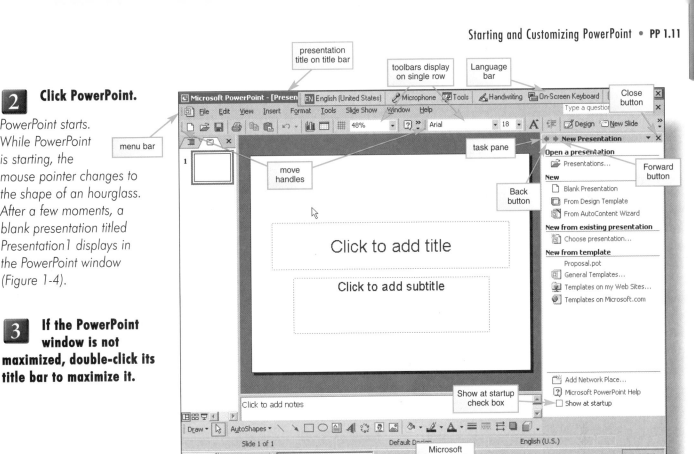

FIGURE 1-4

The screen in Figure 1-4 shows how the PowerPoint window looks the first time you start PowerPoint after installation on most computers. Notice that a task pane displays on the screen and the toolbars display on a single row. A **task pane** is a separate window within the application that provides commonly used commands and enables users to carry out some PowerPoint tasks efficiently. By default, both toolbars display on the same row immediately below the menu bar. Unless the resolution of your display device is greater than 800 × 600, many of the buttons that belong on these toolbars do not display. Hidden buttons display on the **Toolbar Options list**.

In this book, to allow the maximum slide space in the PowerPoint window, the New Presentation task pane that displays at startup is closed. For the most efficient use of the toolbars, the buttons are displayed on two separate rows instead of sharing a single row. You show the toolbar buttons on two rows by clicking the **Show Buttons on Two Rows command** in the Toolbar Options list. You also may display all the buttons on either toolbar by double-clicking the **move handle** on the left side of each toolbar (Figure 1-4). Perform the steps on the next page to customize the PowerPoint window at startup by removing the task pane from the startup instructions and displaying the toolbar buttons on two rows, instead of one.

Other **Ways**

1. Double-click PowerPoint icon on desktop
2. Right-click Start button, click Open All Users, double-click New Office Document, click General tab, double-click Blank Presentation icon
3. On Start menu click New Office Document, click General tab, click New Presentation icon
4. Click New Office Document button on Microsoft Office Shortcut Bar, click General tab, double-click Blank Presentation icon, point to Programs, click Microsoft PowerPoint

Steps **To Customize the PowerPoint Window**

1 **If the New Presentation task pane displays in your PowerPoint window, click the Show at startup check box to remove the check mark, and then click the Close button in the upper-right corner of the task pane title bar (Figure 1-4 on the previous page). If the Language bar displays, point to its Minimize button.**

PowerPoint removes the check mark from the Show at startup check box. PowerPoint will not display the New Presentation task pane the next time PowerPoint starts. The New Presentation task pane closes (Figure 1-5).

FIGURE 1-5

2 **Click the Minimize button on the Language bar. If the toolbars display positioned on the same row, click the Toolbar Options button on the Standard toolbar and then point to Show Buttons on Two Rows.**

The Toolbar Options list displays showing the buttons that do not fit on the toolbars when the buttons display on one row (Figure 1-6).

FIGURE 1-6

3 **Click Show Buttons on Two Rows.**

PowerPoint displays the buttons on the Standard and Formatting toolbars on two separate rows (Figure 1-7). The Toolbar Options list is empty because all the buttons fit on two rows.

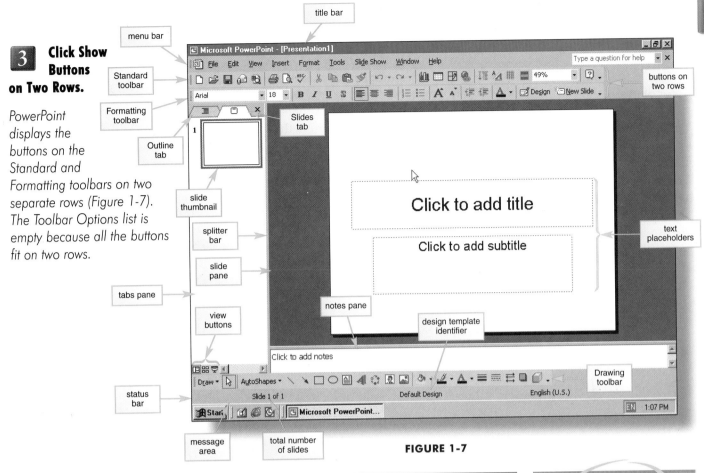

FIGURE 1-7

When you point to a button or other areas on a toolbar, PowerPoint displays a ScreenTip. A **ScreenTip** is a short onscreen note associated with the object to which you are pointing, such as the name of the button. For examples of ScreenTips, see Figure 1-3 on page PP 1.10 and Figure 1-5.

As you work through creating a presentation, you will find that certain PowerPoint operations result in displaying a task pane. Besides the New Presentation task pane shown in Figure 1-4 on page 1.11, PowerPoint provides nine additional task panes: Clipboard, Basic Search, Advanced Search, Slide Layout, Slide Design – Design Templates, Slide Design – Color Schemes, Slide Design – Animation Schemes, Custom Animation, and Slide Transition. These task panes are discussed as they are used. You can display or hide a task pane by clicking the **Task Pane command** on the View menu. You can activate additional task panes by clicking the down arrow to the left of the Close button on the task pane title bar and then selecting a task pane in the list. To switch between task panes, use the Back and Forward buttons on the left side of the task pane title bar.

The PowerPoint Window

The basic unit of a PowerPoint presentation is a **slide**. A slide contains one or many **objects**, such as a title, text, graphics, tables, charts, and drawings. An object is the building block for a PowerPoint slide. PowerPoint assumes the first slide in a new presentation is the **title slide**. The title slide's purpose is to introduce the presentation to the audience.

More About

Task Panes

When you first start PowerPoint, a small window called a task pane may display docked on the right side of the screen. You can drag a task pane title bar to float the pane in your work area or dock it on either the left or right side of a screen, depending on your personal preference.

More *About*

Resolution

Resolution refers to the number of pixels, or dots, that can fit into one square inch. It is measured, consequently, in dots per inch, which is abbreviated, dpi. PowerPoint's default screen resolution is 72 dpi, and it can be set as high as 1,200 dpi. Use a resolution of 150 dpi if you are going to print handouts of your slides. For more information, visit the PowerPoint 2002 More About Web page (scsite.com/ pp2002/more.htm) and then click Resolution.

In PowerPoint, you have the option of using the PowerPoint default settings or establishing your own. A **default setting** is a particular value for a variable that PowerPoint assigns initially. It controls the placement of objects, the color scheme, the transition between slides, and other slide attributes, and it remains in effect unless you cancel or override it. **Attributes** are the properties or characteristics of an object. For example, if you underline the title of a slide, the title is the object, and the underline is the attribute. When you start PowerPoint, the default **slide layout** is **landscape orientation**, where the slide width is greater than its height. In landscape orientation, the slide size is preset to 10 inches wide and 7.5 inches high. You can change the slide layout to **portrait orientation**, so the slide height is greater than its width, by clicking Page Setup on the File menu. In portrait orientation, the slide width is 7.5 inches, and the height is 10 inches.

When a PowerPoint window is open, its name displays in an icon on the Windows taskbar. The **active application** is the one displaying in the foreground of the desktop. That application's corresponding icon on the Windows taskbar displays recessed.

PowerPoint Views

PowerPoint has three main views: normal view, slide sorter view, and slide show view. A **view** is the mode in which the presentation displays on the screen. You may use any or all views when creating a presentation, but you can use only one at a time. You also can select one of these views to be the default view. Change views by clicking one of the view buttons located at the lower-left of the PowerPoint window above the Drawing toolbar (Figure 1-7 on the previous page). The PowerPoint window display varies depending on the view. Some views are graphical while others are textual.

You generally will use normal view and slide sorter view when you are creating a presentation. **Normal view** is composed of three working areas that allow you to work on various aspects of a presentation simultaneously (Figure 1-7). The left side of the screen has a tabs pane that consists of an **Outline tab** and a **Slides tab** that alternate between views of the presentation in an outline of the slide text and a thumbnail, or miniature, view of the slides. You can type the text of the presentation on the Outline tab and easily rearrange bulleted lists, paragraphs, and individual slides. As you type, you can view this text in the **slide pane**, which displays a large view of the current slide on the right side of the window. You also can enter text, graphics, animations, and hyperlinks directly in the slide pane. The **notes pane** at the bottom of the window is an area where you can type notes and additional information. This text can consist of notes to yourself or remarks to share with your audience.

In normal view, you can adjust the width of the slide pane by dragging the **splitter bar** and the height of the notes pane by dragging the pane borders. After you have created at least two slides, **scroll bars**, **scroll arrows**, and **scroll boxes** will display below and to the right of the windows, and you can use them to view different parts of the panes.

Slide sorter view is helpful when you want to see all the slides in the presentation simultaneously. A thumbnail version of each slide displays, and you can rearrange their order, add transitions and timings to switch from one slide to the next in a presentation, add and delete slides, and preview animations.

Slide show view fills the entire screen and allows you to see the slide show just as your audience will view it. Transition effects, animation, graphics, movies, and timings display as they will during an actual presentation.

Table 1-1 identifies the view buttons and provides an explanation of each view.

More *About*

Sizing Panes

The three panes in normal view allow you to work on all aspects of your presentation simultaneously. You can drag the splitter bar and the pane borders to make each area larger or smaller.

Table 1-1	View Buttons and Functions	
BUTTON	**BUTTON NAME**	**FUNCTION**
⊞	Normal View	Displays three panes: the tabs pane with either the Outline tab or the Slides tab, the slide pane, and the notes pane.
⊞⊞	Slide Sorter View	Displays thumbnail versions of all slides in a presentation. You then can copy, cut, paste, or otherwise change the slide position to modify the presentation. Slide sorter view also is used to add timings, to select animated transitions, and to preview animations.
⊟	Slide Show View	Displays the slides as an electronic presentation on the full screen of your computer's monitor. Looking much like a slide projector display, you can see the effect of transitions, build effects, slide timings, and animations.

Placeholders, Text Areas, Mouse Pointer, and Scroll Bars

The PowerPoint window contains elements similar to the document windows in other Microsoft Office applications. Other features are unique to PowerPoint. The main elements are the text placeholders, the mouse pointer, and scroll bars.

PLACEHOLDERS **Placeholders** are boxes that display when you create a new slide. All layouts except the Blank slide layout contain placeholders. Depending on the particular slide layout selected, placeholders display for the slide title, body text, charts, tables, organization charts, media clips, and clip art. You type titles, body text, and bulleted lists in **text placeholders**; you place graphic elements in chart placeholders, table placeholders, organizational chart placeholders, and clip art placeholders. A placeholder is considered an **object**, which is a single element of a slide.

TEXT AREAS **Text areas** are surrounded by a dotted outline. The title slide in Figure 1-7 has two text areas that contain the text placeholders where you will type the main heading, or title, of a new slide and the subtitle, or other object. Other slides in a presentation may use a layout that contains text areas for a title and bulleted lists.

MOUSE POINTER The **mouse pointer** can become one of several different shapes depending on the task you are performing in PowerPoint and the pointer's location on the screen. The different shapes are discussed when they display.

SCROLL BARS When you add a second slide to a presentation, a **vertical scroll bar** displays on the right side of the slide pane. PowerPoint allows you to use the scroll bar to move forward or backward through the presentation.

The **horizontal scroll bar** may display. It is located on the bottom of the slide pane and allows you to display a portion of the slide when the entire slide does not fit on the screen.

Status Bar, Menu Bar, Standard Toolbar, Formatting Toolbar, and Drawing Toolbar

The status bar displays at the bottom of the screen above the Windows taskbar (Figure 1-7). The menu bar, Standard toolbar, and Formatting toolbar display at the top of the screen just below the title bar. The Drawing toolbar displays above the status bar.

Pointing Devices

The Microsoft IntelliMouse® pointing device can help you build presentations efficiently. For example, you can roll the wheel forward or backward instead of clicking a scroll bar. You also can have your document scroll automatically. For more information, visit the PowerPoint 2002 More About Web page (scsite.com/ pp2002/ more.htm) and then click IntelliMouse.

More About

The Default Design Template

Some PowerPoint slide show designers create presentations using the Default Design template. This blank design allows them to concentrate on the words being used to convey the message and does not distract them with colors and various text attributes. Once the text is entered, the designers then select an appropriate design template.

STATUS BAR Immediately above the Windows taskbar at the bottom of the screen is the status bar. The **status bar** consists of a message area and a presentation design template identifier (Figure 1-7 on page PP 1.13). Generally, the message area displays the current slide number and the total number of slides in the slide show. For example, in Figure 1-7 the message area displays Slide 1 of 1. Slide 1 is the current slide, and of 1 indicates the slide show contains only 1 slide. The template identifier displays Default Design, which is the template PowerPoint uses initially.

MENU BAR The **menu bar** is a special toolbar that includes the PowerPoint menu names (Figure 1-8a). Each **menu name** represents a menu of commands that you can use to perform tasks such as retrieving, storing, printing, and manipulating objects in a presentation. When you point to a menu name on the menu bar, the area of the menu bar containing the name changes to a button. To display a menu, such as the Edit menu, click the Edit menu name on the menu bar. A **menu** is a list of commands. If you point to a command on a menu that has an arrow to its right edge, a **submenu** displays another list of commands.

(a) Menu Bar and Toolbars

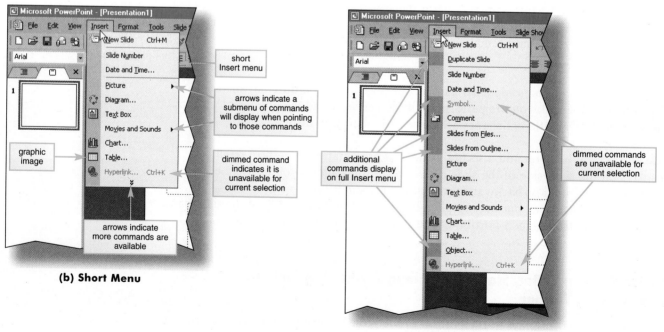

(b) Short Menu

(c) Full Menu

FIGURE 1-8

When you click a menu name on the menu bar, a short menu displays that lists your most recently used commands (Figure 1-8b).

If you wait a few seconds or click the arrows at the bottom of the short menu, it expands into a full menu. A **full menu** lists all the commands associated with a menu (Figure 1-8c). You immediately can display a full menu by double-clicking the menu name on the menu bar. In this book, when you display a menu, always display the full menu using one of these techniques:

1. Click the menu name on the menu bar and then wait a few seconds.
2. Click the menu name on the menu bar and then click the arrows at the bottom of the short menu.
3. Click the menu name on the menu bar and then point to the arrows at the bottom of the short menu.
4. Double-click the menu name on the menu bar.

Both short and full menus display some commands with an image to the left, which associates the command with a graphic image and dimmed commands that appear gray, or dimmed, instead of black, which indicates they are not available for the current selection. A command with a dark gray shading to the left of it on a full menu is called a hidden command because it does not display on a short menu. As you use PowerPoint, it automatically personalizes the short menus for you based on how often you use commands. That is, as you use hidden commands, PowerPoint *unhides* them and places them on the short menu.

The menu bar can change to include other menu names depending on the type of work you are doing in PowerPoint. For example, if you are adding a chart to a slide, Data and Chart menu names are added to the menu bar with commands that reflect charting options.

STANDARD, FORMATTING, AND DRAWING TOOLBARS The Standard toolbar (Figure 1-9a), Formatting toolbar (Figure 1-9b), and Drawing toolbar (Figure 1-9c on the next page) contain buttons and boxes that allow you to perform frequent tasks more quickly than when using the menu bar. For example, to print a slide show, you click the Print button on the Standard toolbar. Each button has an image on the button and a ScreenTip that help you remember the button's function.

Figure 1-9 illustrates the Standard, Formatting, and Drawing toolbars and describes the functions of the buttons. Each of the buttons and boxes are explained in detail when they are used.

FIGURE 1-9a Standard Toolbar

FIGURE 1-9b Formatting Toolbar

FIGURE 1-9c Drawing Toolbar

PowerPoint has several additional toolbars you can display by pointing to Toolbars on the View menu and then clicking the respective name on the Toolbars submenu. You also may display a toolbar by pointing to a toolbar and right-clicking to display a shortcut menu, which lists the available toolbars. A **shortcut menu** contains a list of commands or items that relate to the item to which you are pointing when you right-click.

Speech Recognition

With the **Office Speech Recognition software** installed and a microphone, you can speak the names of toolbar buttons, menus, menu commands, list items, alerts, and dialog box controls, such as OK and Cancel. You also can dictate cell entries, such as text and numbers. To indicate whether you want to speak commands or dictate cell entries, you use the **Language bar** (Figure 1-10a), which also is used for handwriting recognition and for Input Method Editors (IME) that convert keystrokes to East Asian characters. You can display the Language bar in two ways: (1) click the Language Indicator button in the Windows taskbar tray status area by the clock, and then click Show the Language bar on the Language bar menu (Figure 1-10b); or (2) click the **Speech command** on the **Tools menu**.

(a) Language Bar

(b) Language Bar Menu

FIGURE 1-10

If the Language Indicator button does not display in the tray status area, and if the Speech command is not displayed or is dimmed on the Tools menu, the Office Speech Recognition software is not installed. To install the software, you first must start Word and then click Speech on the Tools menu.

If you have speakers, you can instruct the computer to read a slide show to you. By selecting the appropriate option, you can have the slides read in a male or female voice.

Additional information on the Office speech and handwriting recognition capabilities is available in Appendix B.

Choosing a Design Template

A **design template** provides consistency in design and color throughout the entire presentation. It determines the color scheme, font and font size, and layout of a presentation. PowerPoint has three Slide Design task panes that allow you to choose and change the appearance of slides in your presentation. The **Slide Design – Design Templates task pane** displays a variety of styles. You can alter the colors used in the design templates by using the **Slide Design – Color Schemes task pane**. In addition, you can animate elements of your presentation by using the **Slide Design – Animation Schemes task pane**.

In this project, you will select a particular design template by using the Slide Design – Design Templates task pane. The top section of the task pane, labeled Used in This Presentation, displays the template currently used in the slide show. PowerPoint uses the **Default Design** template until you select a different style. When you place your mouse over a template, the name of the template displays. The next section of the task pane is the Recently Used templates. This area displays the four templates you have used in your newest slide shows. The Available For Use area shows additional templates. The templates display in alphabetical order in the two columns.

You want to change the template for this presentation from the Default Design to Proposal. Perform the following steps to apply the Proposal design template.

More About

Additional Templates

While the Slide Design task pane displays a wide variety of templates, more are available in the Microsoft Office Template Gallery at the Microsoft Web site. These templates are arranged in various categories according to the type of presentation.

More About

The PowerPoint Help System

Need Help? It is no further than the Ask a Question box in the upper-right corner of the window. Click the box that contains the text, Type a question for help (Figure 1-8a on page PP 1.16), type help, and then press the ENTER key. PowerPoint will respond with a list of items you can click to learn about obtaining help on any PowerPoint-related topic. To find out what is new in PowerPoint 2002, type what's new in PowerPoint in the Ask a Question box.

Steps **To Choose a Design Template**

1 **Point to the Slide Design button on the Formatting toolbar (Figure 1-11).**

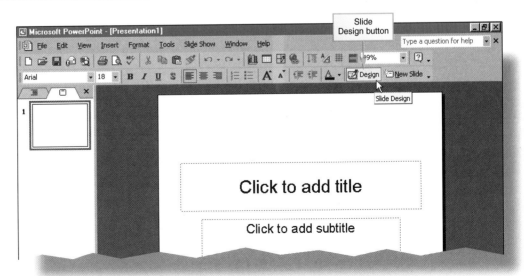

FIGURE 1-11

2 Click the Slide
Design button and
then point to the down
scroll arrow in the Apply
a design template list.

*The Slide Design task pane
displays (Figure 1-12). The
Apply a design template list
displays thumbnail views of
numerous design templates.
Your list may look different
depending on your computer.
The Default Design template
is highlighted in the Used in
This Presentation area. Other
templates display in the
Available For Use area and
possibly in the Recently Used
area. The Close button in the
Slide Design task pane can
be used to close the task
pane if you do not want to
apply a new template.*

FIGURE 1-12

3 Click the down scroll
arrow to scroll
through the list of design
templates until Proposal
displays (row 17, column 1)
in the Available For Use
area. Point to the Proposal
template.

*The proposal template is
selected, as indicated by the
blue box around the template
and the arrow button on the
right side (Figure 1-13).
PowerPoint provides 45 templates in the Available For
Use area. Their names are
listed in alphabetical order.
A ScreenTip displays the
template's name. Your system
may display the ScreenTip,
Proposal.pot, which indicates
the design template's file
extension (.pot).*

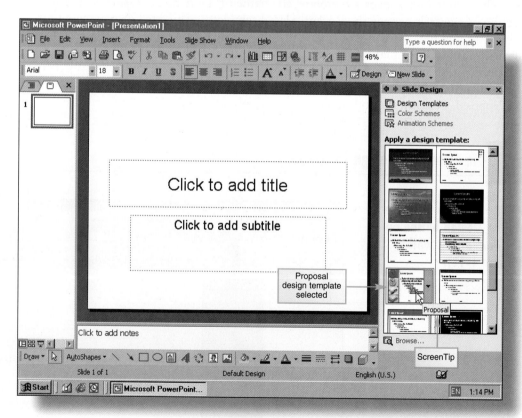

FIGURE 1-13

4 Click Proposal. Point to the Close button in the Slide Design task pane.

The template is applied to Slide 1, as shown in the slide pane and Slides tab (Figure 1-14).

FIGURE 1-14

5 Click the Close button.

Slide 1 displays in normal view with the Proposal design template (Figure 1-15).

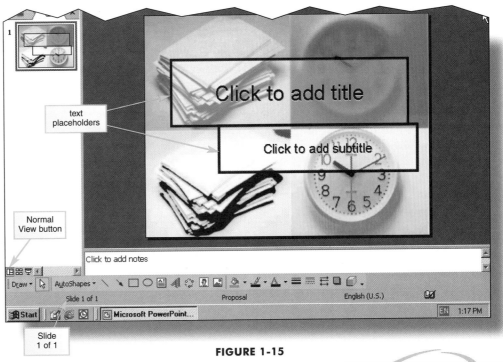

FIGURE 1-15

Other Ways

1. Double-click Proposal in list

Creating a Title Slide

With the exception of a blank slide, PowerPoint assumes every new slide has a title. To make creating a presentation easier, any text you type after a new slide displays becomes title text in the title text placeholder.

Entering the Presentation Title

The presentation title for Project 1 is Time to Start Making Friends. To enter text in your slide, you type on the keyboard or speak into the microphone. As you begin entering text in the title text placeholder, the title text displays immediately in the Slide 1 thumbnail in the Slides tab. Perform the following steps to create the title slide for this presentation.

Steps **To Enter the Presentation Title**

1 **Click the label, Click to add title, located inside the title text placeholder.**

The insertion point is in the title text placeholder (Figure 1-16). The **insertion point** *is a blinking vertical line (|), which indicates where the next character will display. The mouse pointer changes to an I-beam. A* **selection rectangle** *displays around the title text placeholder. The placeholder is selected as indicated by the border and sizing handles displaying on the edges.*

FIGURE 1-16

2 **In the title text placeholder type** Time to Start **and then press the ENTER key. Type** Making Friends **but do not press the ENTER key.**

The title text, Time to Start Making Friends, displays on two lines in the title text placeholder and in the Slides tab (Figure 1-17). The insertion point displays after the letter s in Friends. The title text displays centered in the placeholder with the default text attributes: Arial font, font size 54, and shadow effect.

FIGURE 1-17

Other Ways

1. In Dictation mode, say "Time to start, New Line, Making friends"

PowerPoint **line wraps** text that exceeds the width of the placeholder. One of PowerPoint's features is **text AutoFit**. If you are creating a slide and need to squeeze an extra line in the text placeholder, PowerPoint will prompt you to resize the existing text in the placeholder so the spillover text will fit on the slide.

Correcting a Mistake When Typing

If you type the wrong letter, press the BACKSPACE key to erase all the characters back to and including the one that is incorrect. If you mistakenly press the ENTER key after typing the title and the insertion point is on the new line, simply press the BACKSPACE key to return the insertion point to the right of the letter s in the word Friends.

When you install PowerPoint, the default setting allows you to reverse up to the last 20 changes by clicking the **Undo button** on the Standard toolbar. The ScreenTip that displays when you point to the Undo button changes to indicate the type of change just made. For example, if you type text in the title text placeholder and then point to the Undo button, the ScreenTip that displays is Undo Typing. For clarity, when referencing the Undo button in this project, the name displaying in the ScreenTip is referenced. Another way to reverse changes is to click the **Undo command** on the Edit menu. As with the Undo button, the Undo command reflects the last type of change made to the presentation.

You can reapply a change that you reversed with the Undo button by clicking the **Redo button** on the Standard toolbar. Clicking the Redo button reverses the last undo action. The ScreenTip name reflects the type of reversal last preformed.

Entering the Presentation Subtitle

The next step in creating the title slide is to enter the subtitle text into the subtitle text placeholder. Complete the steps on the next page to enter the presentation subtitle.

More About

The 7 × 7 Rule

All slide shows in the projects and exercises in this book follow the 7 × 7 rule. This guideline states that each slide should have a maximum of seven lines, and each of these lines should have a maximum of seven words. This rule requires PowerPoint designers to choose their words carefully and, in turn, helps viewers read the slides easily.

Steps **To Enter the Presentation Subtitle**

1 **Click the label, Click to add subtitle, located inside the subtitle text placeholder.**

The insertion point displays in the subtitle text placeholder (Figure 1-18). The mouse pointer changes to an I-beam indicating the mouse is in a text placeholder. The selection rectangle indicates the placeholder is selected.

FIGURE 1-18

2 **Type** Presented by **and then press the ENTER key. Type** Westview College Counselors **but do not press the ENTER key.**

The subtitle text displays in the subtitle text placeholder and the Slides tab (Figure 1-19). The insertion point displays after the letter s in Counselors. A red wavy line displays below the word, Westview, to indicate a possible spelling error.

Other **Ways**

1. In Dictation mode, say "Presented by, New Line, Westview College Counselors"

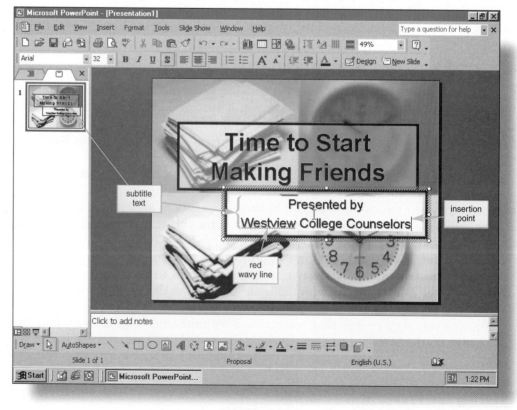

FIGURE 1-19

After pressing the ENTER key in Step 2, PowerPoint created a new line, which is the second paragraph in the placeholder. A **paragraph** is a segment of text with the same format that begins when you press the ENTER key and ends when you press the ENTER key again.

Text Attributes

This presentation uses the Proposal design template. Each design template has its own text attributes. A **text attribute** is a characteristic of the text, such as font, font size, font style, or text color. You can adjust text attributes any time before, during, or after you type the text. Recall that a design template determines the color scheme, font and font size, and layout of a presentation. Most of the time, you use the design template's text attributes and color scheme. Occasionally, you may want to change the way a presentation looks, however, and still keep a particular design template. PowerPoint gives you that flexibility. You can use the design template and change the font and the font's color, effects, size, and style. Text may have one or more font styles and effects simultaneously. Table 1-2 explains the different text attributes available in PowerPoint.

The next two sections explain how to change the font size and font style attributes.

More About

Modifying Fonts

Designers recommend using a maximum of two fonts and two font styles or effects in a slide show. This design philosophy maintains balance and simplicity.

Table 1-2	Design Template Text Attributes
ATTRIBUTE	*DESCRIPTION*
Color	Defines the color of text. Displaying text in color requires a color monitor. Printing text in color requires a color printer or plotter.
Effects	Effects include underline, shadow, emboss, superscript, and subscript. Effects can be applied to most fonts.
Font	Defines the appearance and shape of letters, numbers, and special characters.
Size	Specifies the height of characters on the screen. Character size is gauged by a measurement system called points. A single point is about 1/72 of an inch in height. Thus, a character with a point size of 18 is about 18/72 (or 1/4) of an inch in height.
Style	Font styles include regular, bold, italic, and bold italic.

Changing the Style of Text to Italic

Text font styles include plain, italic, bold, shadowed, and underlined. PowerPoint allows you to use one or more text font styles in a presentation. Perform the steps on the next page to add emphasis to the first line of the subtitle text by changing regular text to italic text.

Steps **To Change the Text Font Style to Italic**

1 **Triple-click the paragraph, Westview College Counselors, in the subtitle text placeholder, and then point to the Italic button on the Formatting toolbar.**

*The paragraph, Westview College Counselors, is highlighted (Figure 1-20). The **Italic button** is surrounded by a blue box. You select an entire paragraph quickly by triple-clicking any text within the paragraph.*

FIGURE 1-20

2 **Click the Italic button.**

The text is italicized on the slide and the slide thumbnail (Figure 1-21).

Other Ways

1. Right-click selected text, click Font on shortcut menu, click Italic in Font style list
2. On Format menu click Font, click Italic in Font style list
3. Press CTRL+I
4. In Voice Command mode, say "Italic"

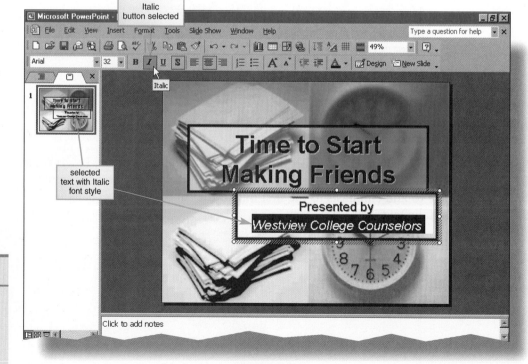

FIGURE 1-21

To remove the italic style from text, select the italicized text and then click the Italic button. As a result, the Italic button is not selected, and the text does not have the italic font style.

Changing the Font Size

The Proposal design template default font size is 54 point for title text and 32 point for body text. A point is 1/72 of an inch in height. Thus, a character with a point size of 54 is 54/72 (or 3/4) of an inch in height. Slide 1 requires you to increase the font size for the paragraph, Presented by. Perform the following steps to increase the font size.

Steps **To Increase Font Size**

1 **Position the mouse pointer in the paragraph, Presented by, and then triple-click.**

PowerPoint selects the entire paragraph (Figure 1-22).

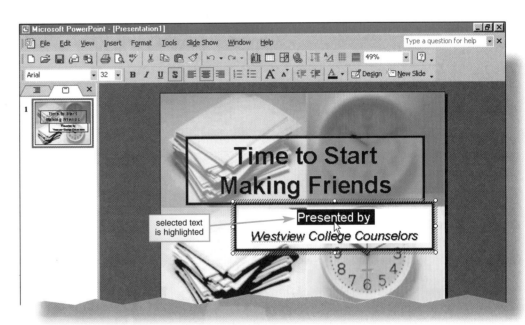

FIGURE 1-22

2 **Point to the Font Size box arrow on the Formatting toolbar.**

*The ScreenTip displays the words, Font Size (Figure 1-23). The **Font Size box** is surrounded by a blue box and indicates that the subtitle text is 32 point.*

FIGURE 1-23

Click the Font Size box arrow, click the Font Size box scroll bar one time, and then point to 40 in the Font Size list.

When you click the *Font Size box arrow*, a list of available font sizes displays in the Font Size list (Figure 1-24). The font sizes displayed depend on the current font, which is Arial. Font size 40 is highlighted.

FIGURE 1-24

 Click 40.

The font size of the subtitle text, *Presented by*, increases to 40 point (Figure 1-25). The Font Size box on the Formatting toolbar displays 40, indicating the selected text has a font size of 40.

FIGURE 1-25

Other Ways

1. Click Increase Font Size button on Formatting toolbar
2. On Format menu click Font, click new font size in Size box, or type font size between 1 and 4000, click OK button
3. Right-click selected text, click Font on shortcut menu, type new font size in Size box, click OK button
4. In Voice Command mode, say "Font Size, [font size]"

The **Increase Font Size button** on the Formatting toolbar (Figure 1-25) increases the font size in preset increments each time you click the button. If you need to decrease the font size, click the Font Size box arrow and then select a size smaller than 32. The **Decrease Font Size button** on the Formatting toolbar (Figure 1-25) also decreases the font size in preset increments each time you click the button.

Saving the Presentation on a Floppy Disk

While you are building a presentation, the computer stores it in memory. It is important to save the presentation frequently because the presentation will be lost if the computer is turned off or you lose electrical power. Another reason to save your work is that if you run out of lab time before completing your project, you may finish the project later without starting over. Therefore, always save any presentation you will use later. Before you continue with Project 1, save the work completed thus far. Perform the following steps to save a presentation on a floppy disk using the Save button on the Standard toolbar.

> **More About**
>
> ### Text Attributes
>
> The Microsoft Web site contains a comprehensive glossary of typography terms. The information includes a diagram illustrating text attributes. For more information, visit the PowerPoint 2002 More About Web page (scsite.com/pp2002/more.htm) and then click Attributes.

 To Save a Presentation on a Floppy Disk

1 **Insert a formatted floppy disk in drive A. Click the Save button on the Standard toolbar.**

The Save As dialog box displays (Figure 1-26). The default folder, My Documents, displays in the Save in box. Time to Start Making Friends displays highlighted in the File name text box because PowerPoint uses the words in the title text placeholder as the default file name. Presentation displays in the Save as type box. Clicking the Cancel button closes the Save As dialog box.

FIGURE 1-26

2 **Type** Make Friends **in the File name text box. Do not press the** ENTER **key after typing the file name. Point to the Save in box arrow.**

The name, Make Friends, displays in the File name text box (Figure 1-27).

FIGURE 1-27

3 **Click the Save in box arrow. Point to 3½ Floppy (A:) in the Save in list.**

The Save in list displays a list of locations in which to save a presentation; 3½ Floppy (A:) is highlighted (Figure 1-28). Your list may look different depending on the configuration of your system.

FIGURE 1-28

4 Click 3½ Floppy (A:) and then point to the Save button in the Save As dialog box.

Drive A becomes the current drive (Figure 1-29).

FIGURE 1-29

5 Click the Save button.

PowerPoint saves the presentation on the floppy disk in drive A. The title bar displays the file name used to save the presentation, Make Friends (Figure 1-30).

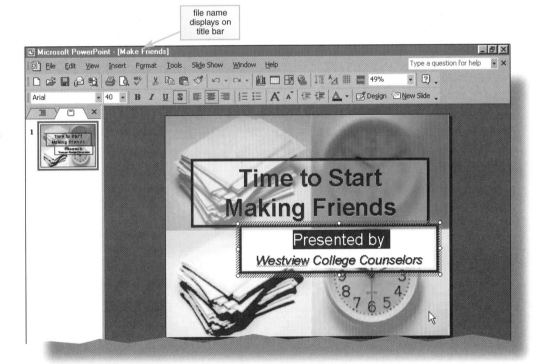

FIGURE 1-30

PowerPoint automatically appends the extension .ppt to the file name, Make Friends. The **.ppt** extension stands for **PowerPoint**. Although the slide show, Make Friends, is saved on a floppy disk, it also remains in memory and displays on the screen.

Other Ways

1. On File menu click Save As
2. Press CTRL+S or press SHIFT+F12
3. In Voice Command mode, say "File, Save As, [type file name], Save"

It is a good practice to save periodically while you are working on a project. By doing so, you protect yourself from losing all the work you have done since the last time you saved.

Adding a New Slide to a Presentation

With the title slide for the presentation created, the next step is to add the first text slide immediately after the title slide. Usually, when you create a presentation, you add slides with text, graphics, or charts. When you add a new slide, PowerPoint uses the Title and Text slide layout. Some placeholders allow you to double-click the placeholder and then access other objects, such as media clips, charts, diagrams, and organization charts.

Perform the following steps to add a new Text slide layout with a bulleted list.

Steps To Add a New Text Slide with a Bulleted List

1 **Click to the New Slide button on the Formatting toolbar (Figure 1-31).**

The Slide Layout task pane opens. The Title and Text slide layout is selected. Slide 2 of 2 displays on the status bar.

FIGURE 1-31

2 Click the Show when inserting new slides check box to remove the check mark. Click the Close button on the Slide Layout task pane.

Slide 2 displays in both the slide pane and Slides tab retaining the attributes of the Proposal design template (Figure 1-32). The vertical scroll bar displays in the slide pane. The bullet displays as a square.

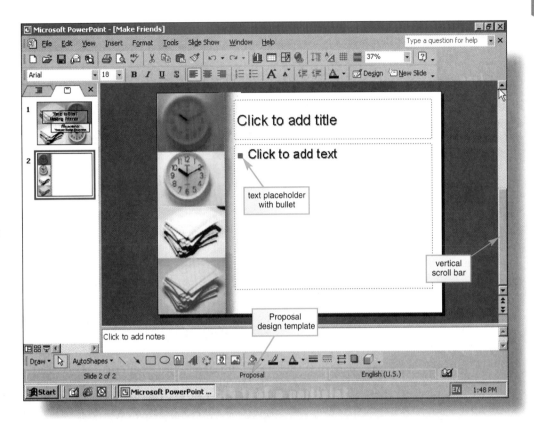

FIGURE 1-32

Slide 2 displays with a title text placeholder and a text placeholder with a bullet. You can change the layout for a slide at any time during the creation of a presentation by clicking Format on the menu bar and then clicking Slide Layout. You also can click View on the menu bar and then click Task Pane. You then can double-click the slide layout of your choice from the Slide Layout task pane.

Creating a Text Slide with a Single-Level Bulleted List

The information in the Slide 2 text placeholder is presented in a bulleted list. All the bullets display on one level. A **level** is a position within a structure, such as an outline, that indicates the magnitude of importance. PowerPoint allows for five paragraph levels. Each paragraph level has an associated bullet. The bullet font is dependent on the design template.

Entering a Slide Title

PowerPoint assumes every new slide has a title. The title for Slide 2 is Meet People. Perform the step on the next page to enter this title.

Steps **To Enter a Slide Title**

1 **Type** Meet People **in the title text placeholder. Do not press the ENTER key.**

The title, Meet People, displays in the title text placeholder and in the Slides tab (Figure 1-33). The insertion point displays after the e in People. The selection rectangle indicates the title text placeholder is selected.

FIGURE 1-33

Other Ways

1. In Dictation mode, say "Meet People"

Selecting a Text Placeholder

Before you can type text into the text placeholder, you first must select it. Perform the following step to select the text placeholder on Slide 2.

Steps **To Select a Text Placeholder**

1 **Click the bulleted paragraph labeled, Click to add text.**

The insertion point displays immediately to the right of the bullet on Slide 2 (Figure 1-34). The mouse pointer may change shape if you move it away from the bullet. The selection rectangle indicates the text placeholder is selected.

FIGURE 1-34

Other Ways

1. Press CTRL+ENTER

Typing a Single-Level Bulleted List

As discussed previously, a bulleted list is a list of paragraphs, each of which is preceded by a bullet. A paragraph is a segment of text ended by pressing the ENTER key. The next step is to type the single-level bulleted list, which consists of four entries (Figure 1-2b on page PP 1.09). Perform the following steps to type a single-level bulleted list.

Steps | To Type a Single-Level Bulleted List

1 **Type** Develop confidence to introduce yourself to others **and then press the** **ENTER key.**

The paragraph, Develop confidence to introduce yourself to others, displays (Figure 1-35). The font size is 32. The insertion point displays after the second bullet. When you press the ENTER key, PowerPoint ends one paragraph and begins a new paragraph. With the Text slide layout, PowerPoint places a pink square bullet in front of the new paragraph.

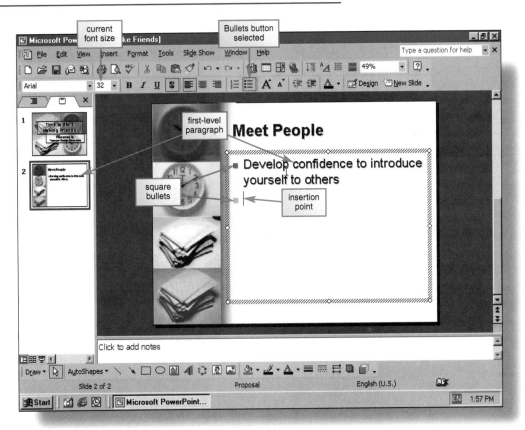

FIGURE 1-35

2 **Type** Make eye contact **and then press the ENTER key. Type** Smile and say, "Hi" **and then press the ENTER key. Type** Do not wait; start early in the semester **but do not press the ENTER key. Point to the New Slide button on the Formatting toolbar.**

The insertion point displays after the r in semester (Figure 1-36). Three new first-level paragraphs display with square bullets in both the text placeholder and the Slides tab. When you press the ENTER key, PowerPoint adds a new paragraph at the same level as the previous paragraph.

FIGURE 1-36

Notice that you did not press the ENTER key after typing the last paragraph in Step 2. If you press the ENTER key, a new bullet displays after the last entry on this slide. To remove an extra bullet, press the BACKSPACE key.

Creating a Text Slide with a Multi-Level Bulleted List

Slides 3 and 4 in Figure 1-2 on page PP 1.09 contain more than one level of bulleted text. A slide that consists of more than one level of bulleted text is called a **multi-level bulleted list slide**. Beginning with the second level, each paragraph indents to the right of the preceding level and is pushed down to a lower level. For example, if you increase the indent of a first-level paragraph, it becomes a second-level paragraph. This lower-level paragraph is a subset of the higher-level paragraph. It usually contains information that supports the topic in the paragraph immediately above it. You increase the indent of a paragraph by clicking the **Increase Indent button** on the Formatting toolbar.

When you want to raise a paragraph from a lower level to a higher level, you click the **Decrease Indent button** on the Formatting toolbar.

Creating a text slide with a multi-level bulleted list requires several steps. Initially, you enter a slide title in the title text placeholder. Next, you select the body text placeholder. Then, you type the text for the multi-level bulleted list, increasing and decreasing the indents as needed. The next several sections explain how to add a slide with a multi-level bulleted list.

Adding New Slides and Entering Slide Titles

When you add a new slide to a presentation, PowerPoint keeps the same layout used on the previous slide. PowerPoint assumes every new slide has a title. The title for Slide 3 is Find the Right Places. Perform the following steps to add a new slide (Slide 3) and enter a title.

Steps | To Add a New Slide and Enter a Slide Title

1 **Click the New Slide button.**

Slide 3 of 3 displays in the slide pane and Slides tab (Figure 1-37).

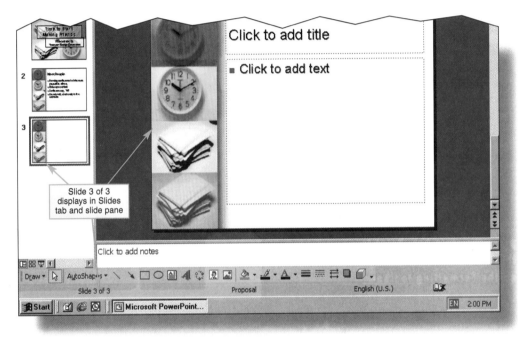

FIGURE 1-37

2 **Type** Find the Right Places **in the title text placeholder. Do not press the ENTER key.**

Slide 3 displays the Text slide layout with the title, Find the Right Places, in the title text placeholder and in the Slides tab (Figure 1-38). The insertion point displays after the s in Places.

FIGURE 1-38

Slide 3 is added to the presentation with the desired title.

Other Ways

1. Press SHIFT+CTRL+M
2. In Dictation mode, say "New Slide, Find the right places"

Typing a Multi-Level Bulleted List

The next step is to select the body text placeholder and then type the multi-level bulleted list, which consists of five entries (Figure 1-2c on page PP 1.09). Perform the following steps to create a list consisting of three levels.

Steps **To Type a Multi-Level Bulleted List**

1 **Click the bulleted paragraph labeled, Click to add text.**

The insertion point displays immediately to the right of the bullet on Slide 3. The mouse pointer may change shape if you move it away from the bullet.

2 **Type** Go where people congregate **and then press the ENTER key. Point to the Increase Indent button on the Formatting toolbar.**

The paragraph, Go where people congregate, displays (Figure 1-39). The font size is 32. The insertion point displays to the right of the second bullet.

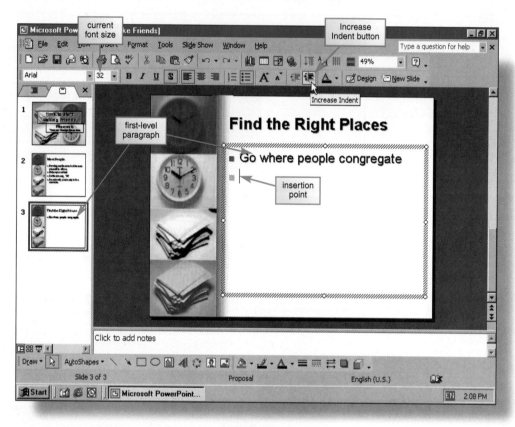

FIGURE 1-39

3 **Click the Increase Indent button.**

The second paragraph indents below the first and becomes a second-level paragraph (Figure 1-40). The bullet to the left of the second paragraph changes from a square to a circle, and the font size for the paragraph now is 28. The insertion point displays to the right of the circle.

FIGURE 1-40

4 **Type** Student union, sports events **and then press the ENTER key. Point to the Decrease Indent button on the Formatting toolbar.**

The first second-level paragraph displays with a brown circle bullet in both the slide pane and the Slides tab (Figure 1-41). When you press the ENTER key, PowerPoint adds a new paragraph at the same level as the previous paragraph.

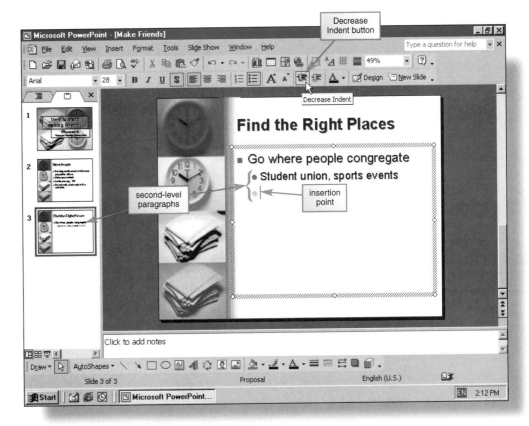

FIGURE 1-41

5 **Click the Decrease Indent button.**

The second-level paragraph becomes a first-level paragraph (Figure 1-42). The bullet of the new paragraph changes from a circle to a square, and the font size for the paragraph is 32. The insertion point displays to the right of the square bullet.

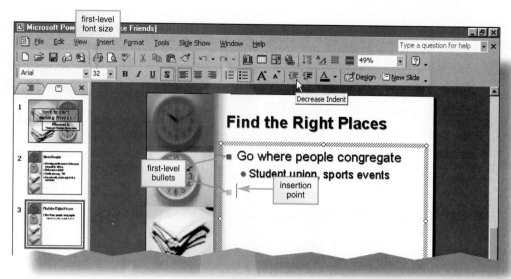

FIGURE 1-42

Perform the following steps to complete the text for Slide 3.

TO TYPE THE REMAINING TEXT FOR SLIDE 3

1 Type Get involved in extracurricular activities and then press the ENTER key.

2 Click the Increase Indent button on the Formatting toolbar.

3 Type Participate in intramurals and then press the ENTER key.

4 Type Join Student Government but do not press the ENTER key.

Slide 3 displays as shown in Figure 1-43. The insertion point displays after the t in Government.

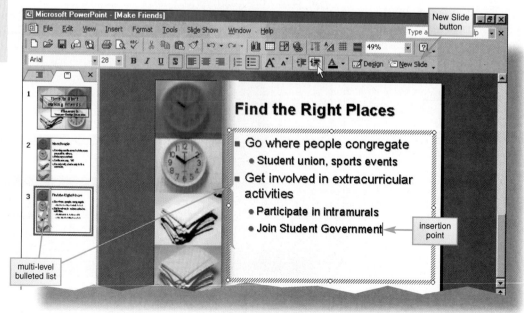

FIGURE 1-43

In Step 4 above, you did not press the ENTER key after typing the last paragraph. If you press the ENTER key, a new bullet displays after the last entry on this slide. To remove an extra bullet, press the BACKSPACE key.

Slide 4 is the last slide in this presentation. It also is a multi-level bulleted list and has three levels. Perform the following steps to create Slide 4.

TO CREATE SLIDE 4

1 Click the New Slide button on the Formatting toolbar.

2 Type Start a Conversation in the title text placeholder.

3 Press CTRL+ENTER to move the insertion point to the body text placeholder.

4 Type Talk about almost anything and then press the ENTER key.

5 Click the Increase Indent button on the Formatting toolbar. Type Comment on what is going on and then press the ENTER key.

The title and first two levels of bullets are added to Slide 4 (Figure 1-44).

Creating a Third-Level Paragraph

The next line in Slide 4 is indented an additional level to the third level. Perform the following steps to create an additional level.

Steps **To Create a Third-Level Paragraph**

1 **Click the Increase Indent button on the Formatting toolbar.**

The second-level paragraph becomes a third-level paragraph (Figure 1-44). The bullet to the left of the new paragraph changes from a circle to a square, and the font size for the paragraph is 24. The insertion point displays after the square bullet.

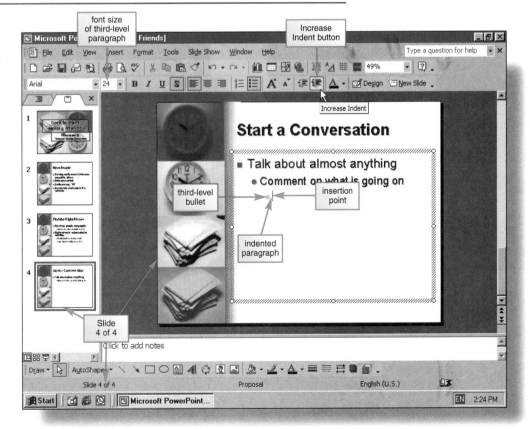

FIGURE 1-44

> **Other Ways**
>
> 1. In Dictation mode, say "New Slide, Start a conversation, New, Talk about almost anything, New Line, Tab, Comment on what is going on"

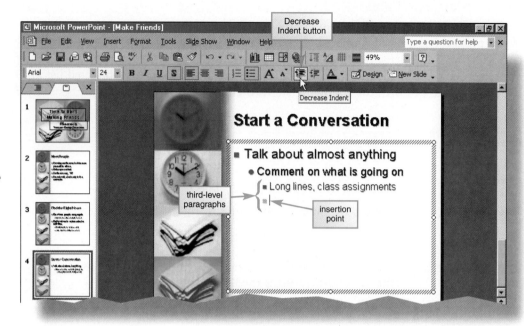

2 **Type** Long lines, class assignments **and then press the ENTER key. Point to the Decrease Indent button on the Formatting toolbar.**

The first third-level paragraph, Long lines, class assignments, displays with the bullet for a second third-level paragraph (Figure 1-45).

FIGURE 1-45

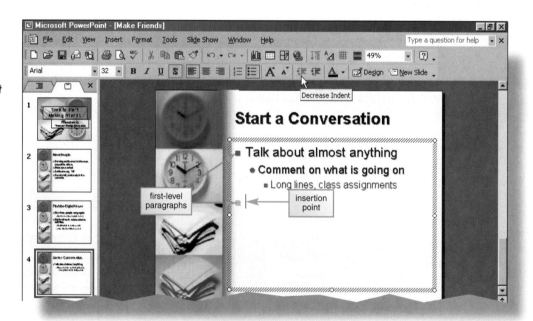

3 **Click the Decrease Indent button two times.**

The insertion point displays at the first level (Figure 1-46).

FIGURE 1-46

The title text and three levels of paragraphs discussing conversation topics are complete. The next three paragraphs concern the types of questions to ask. As an alternative to clicking the Increase Indent button, you can press the TAB key. Likewise, instead of clicking the Decrease Indent button, you can press the SHIFT+TAB keys. Perform the following steps to type the remaining text for Slide 4.

TO TYPE THE REMAINING TEXT FOR SLIDE 4

1 Type Ask questions and then press the ENTER key.

2 Press the TAB key to increase the indent to the second level.

3 Type Get people to discuss their lives and then press the ENTER key.

4 Press the TAB key to increase the indent to the third level.

5 Type Hobbies, classes, and work but do not press the ENTER key.

Other Ways

1. In Dictation mode, say "Ask questions, New Line, Tab, Get people to discuss their lives, New Line, Tab, Hobbies comma classes comma and work"

The Slide 4 title text and body text display in the slide pane and Slides tabs (Figure 1-47). The insertion point displays after the k in work.

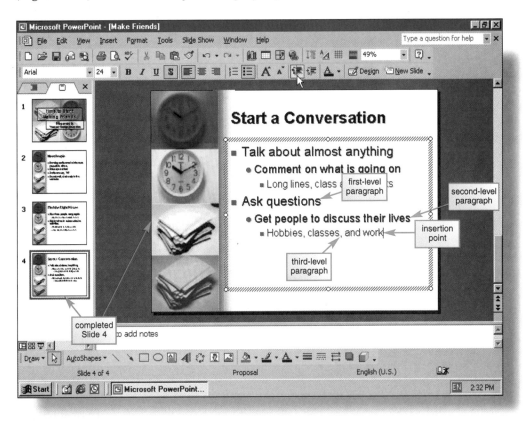

FIGURE 1-47

All the slides are created for the Make Friends slide show. This presentation consists of a title slide and three text slides with a multi-level bulleted list.

Ending a Slide Show with a Black Slide

After the last slide in the slide show displays, the default PowerPoint setting is to end the presentation with a black slide. This black slide displays only when the slide show is running and concludes the slide show gracefully so your audience never sees the PowerPoint window. A **black slide** ends all slide shows unless the option setting is deselected. Perform the steps on the next page to verify the End with black slide option is activated.

More About

More About Black Slides

Black slides can be used effectively to end a presentation, to pause for discussion, or to separate sections of a large presentation. The black slide focuses the audience's attention on you, the speaker, and away from the screen display.

Steps **To End a Slide Show with a Black Slide**

1 Click Tools on the menu bar and then point to Options (Figure 1-48).

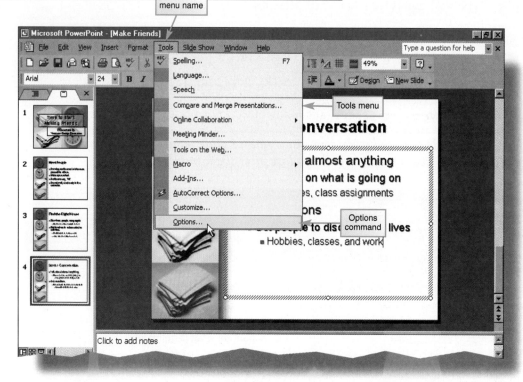

FIGURE 1-48

2 Click Options. If necessary, click the View tab when the Options dialog box displays. Verify that the End with black slide check box is selected. If a check mark does not display, click End with black slide, and then point to the OK button.

The Options dialog box displays (Figure 1-49). The View sheet contains settings for the overall PowerPoint display and for a particular slide show.

3 Click the OK button.

The End with black slide option will cause the slide show to end with a black slide until it is deselected.

FIGURE 1-49

With all aspects of the presentation complete, it is important to save the additions and changes you have made to the Make Friends presentation.

Saving a Presentation with the Same File Name

Saving frequently cannot be overemphasized. When you first saved the presentation, you clicked the Save button on the Standard toolbar and the Save dialog box displayed. When you want to save the changes made to the presentation after your last save, you again click the Save button. This time, however, the Save dialog box does not display because PowerPoint updates the document called Make Friends.ppt on the floppy disk. Perform the following steps to save the presentation again.

TO SAVE A PRESENTATION WITH THE SAME FILE NAME

1 Be sure your floppy disk is in drive A.

2 Click the Save button on the Standard toolbar.

PowerPoint overwrites the old Make Friends.ppt document on the floppy disk in drive A with the revised presentation document. Slide 4 displays in the PowerPoint window.

Other Ways

1. In Voice Command mode, say "Save"

Moving to Another Slide in Normal View

When creating or editing a presentation in normal view, you often want to display a slide other than the current one. You can move to another slide using several methods. In the Outline tab, you can point to any of the text in a particular slide to display that slide in the slide pane, or you can drag the scroll box on the vertical scroll bar up or down to move through the text in the presentation. In the slide pane, you can click the Previous Slide or Next Slide button on the vertical scroll bar. Clicking the **Next Slide button** advances to the next slide in the presentation. Clicking the **Previous Slide button** backs up to the slide preceding the current slide. You also can drag the scroll box on the vertical scroll bar. When you drag the scroll box, the **slide indicator** displays the number and title of the slide you are about to display. Releasing the mouse button displays the slide.

A slide's **Zoom setting** affects the portion of the slide displaying in the slide pane. PowerPoint defaults to a setting of approximately 50 percent so the entire slide displays. This percentage depends on the size and type of your monitor. If you want to display a small portion of the current slide, you would zoom in by clicking the **Zoom box arrow** and then clicking the desired magnification. You can display the entire slide in the slide pane by clicking **Fit** in the Zoom list. The Zoom setting affects the action of the vertical and horizontal scroll bars. If Zoom is set so the entire slide is not visible in the slide pane, clicking the up scroll arrow on the vertical scroll bar displays the next portion of the slide, not the previous slide.

More About

Zoom Settings

You can increase your Zoom setting as large as 400% when you want to see details on small objects. Likewise, you can decrease your Zoom setting as small as 10%. When you want to redisplay the entire slide, click Fit in the Zoom list.

Using the Scroll Box on the Slide Pane to Move to Another Slide

Before continuing with Project 1, you want to display the title slide. Perform the steps on the next page to move from Slide 4 to Slide 1 using the scroll box on the slide pane vertical scroll bar.

To Use the Scroll Box on the Slide Pane to Move to Another Slide

1 Position the mouse pointer on the scroll box. Press and hold down the mouse button.

Slide: 4 of 4 Start a Conversation displays in the slide indicator (Figure 1-50). When you click the scroll box, the Slide 4 thumbnail is not shaded in the Slides tab.

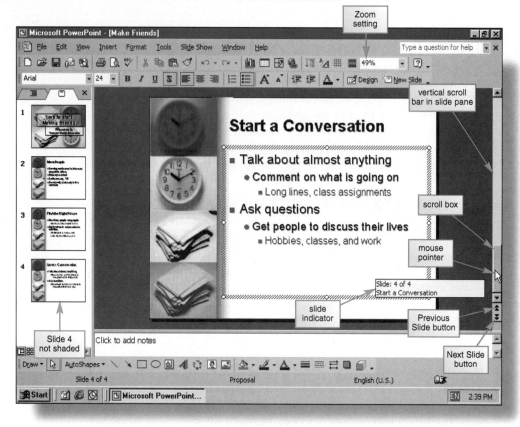

FIGURE 1-50

2 Drag the scroll box up the vertical scroll bar until Slide: 1 of 4 Time to Start Making Friends displays in the slide indicator.

Slide: 1 of 4 Time to Start Making Friends displays in the slide indicator (Figure 1-51). Slide 4 still displays in the PowerPoint window.

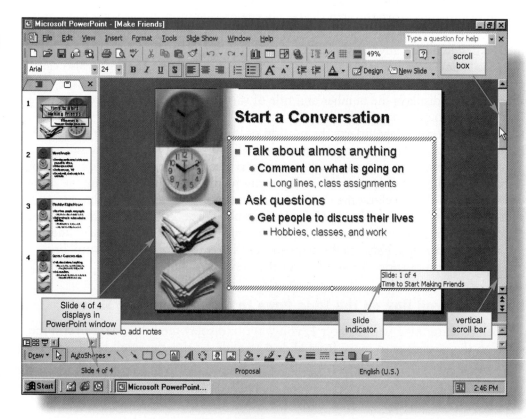

FIGURE 1-51

3 **Release the mouse button.**

Slide 1, titled Time to Start Making Friends, displays in the PowerPoint window (Figure 1-52). The Slide 1 thumbnail is shaded in the Slides tab indicating it is selected.

FIGURE 1-52

Viewing the Presentation in Slide Show View

The **Slide Show button**, located at the lower-left of the PowerPoint window above the status bar, allows you to display a presentation electronically using a computer. The computer acts like a slide projector, displaying each slide on a full screen. The full screen slide hides the toolbars, menus, and other PowerPoint window elements. When making a presentation, you use **slide show view**. You can start slide show view from normal view or slide sorter view.

Starting Slide Show View

Slide show view begins when you click the Slide Show button at the lower-left of the PowerPoint window above the status bar. PowerPoint then displays the current slide on the full screen without any of the PowerPoint window objects, such as the menu bar or toolbars. Perform the steps on the next page to start slide show view.

Other Ways

1. Click Next Slide button or Previous Slide button to move forward or back one slide

2. Press PAGE DOWN or PAGE UP to move forward or back one slide

3. In Voice Command mode, say "Next page" or "Previous page"

To Start Slide Show View

1 **Point to the Slide Show button in the lower-left corner of the PowerPoint window above the status bar (Figure 1-53).**

FIGURE 1-53

2 **Click the Slide Show button.**

A starting slide show message displays momentarily and then the title slide fills the screen (Figure 1-54). The PowerPoint window is hidden.

FIGURE 1-54

Advancing Through a Slide Show Manually

After you begin slide show view, you can move forward or backward through the slides. PowerPoint allows you to advance through the slides manually or automatically. Perform the following steps to move manually through the slides.

 Steps To Move Manually Through Slides in a Slide Show

1 **Click each slide until the Start a Conversation slide (Slide 4) displays.**

Slide 4 displays (Figure 1-55). Each slide in the presentation displays on the screen, one slide at a time. Each time you click the mouse button, the next slide displays.

Slide 4 displays in slide show view

Start a Conversation

- Talk about almost anything
  - Comment on what is going on
    - Long lines, class assignments
- Ask questions
  - Get people to discuss their lives
    - Hobbies, classes, and work

FIGURE 1-55

2 **Click Slide 4.**

The black slide displays (Figure 1-56). The message at the top of the slide announces the end of the slide show. If you wanted to end the presentation at this point and return to normal view, you would click the black slide.

End of slide show, click to exit.

message

FIGURE 1-56

Using the Popup Menu to Go to a Specific Slide

Slide show view has a shortcut menu, called the **Popup menu**, that displays when you right-click a slide in slide show view. This menu contains commands to assist you during a slide show. For example, clicking the **Next command** moves to the next

Other Ways

1. Press PAGE DOWN to advance one slide at a time, or press PAGE UP to go backward one slide at a time

2. Press RIGHT ARROW to advance one slide at a time, or press LEFT ARROW key to go back one slide at a time

slide. Clicking the **Previous command** moves to the previous slide. Pointing to the **Go command** and then clicking Slide Navigator allows you to move to any slide in the presentation. The **Slide Navigator dialog box** contains a list of the slides in the presentation. Go to the requested slide by double-clicking the name of that slide. Perform the following steps to go to the title slide (Slide 1) in the Make Friends presentation.

Steps **To Display the Popup Menu and Go to a Specific Slide**

1 **With the black slide displaying in slide show view, right-click the slide. Point to Go on the Popup menu, and then point to Slide Navigator on the Go submenu.**

The Popup menu displays on the black slide, and the Go submenu displays (Figure 1-57). Your screen may look different because the Popup menu displays near the location of the mouse pointer at the time you right-click.

FIGURE 1-57

2 **Click Slide Navigator. When the Slide Navigator dialog box displays, point to 1. Time to Start Making Friends in the Slide titles list.**

The Slide Navigator dialog box contains a list of the slides in the presentation (Figure 1-58).

3 **Double-click 1. Time to Start Making Friends.**

The title slide, Time to Start Making Friends (shown in Figure 1-54 on page PP 1.48), displays.

FIGURE 1-58

Other **Ways**

1. Right-click slide, point to Go on Popup menu, click Slide Navigator, type slide number, press ENTER

Additional Popup menu commands allow you to write meeting minutes or to create a list of action items during a slide show, change the mouse pointer to a pen that draws in various colors, blacken the screen, and end the slide show. Popup menu commands are discussed as they are used.

Using the Popup Menu to End a Slide Show

The **End Show command** on the Popup menu ends slide show view and returns to the same view as when you clicked the Slide Show button. Perform the following steps to end slide show view and return to normal view.

 To Use the Popup Menu to End a Slide Show

1 **Right-click the title slide and then point to End Show on the Popup menu.**

The Popup menu displays on Slide 1 (Figure 1-59).

2 **Click End Show. If the Microsoft PowerPoint dialog box displays, click the Yes button.**

PowerPoint ends slide show view and returns to normal view (shown in Figure 1-60 on the next page). Slide 1 displays because it is the last slide displayed in slide show view.

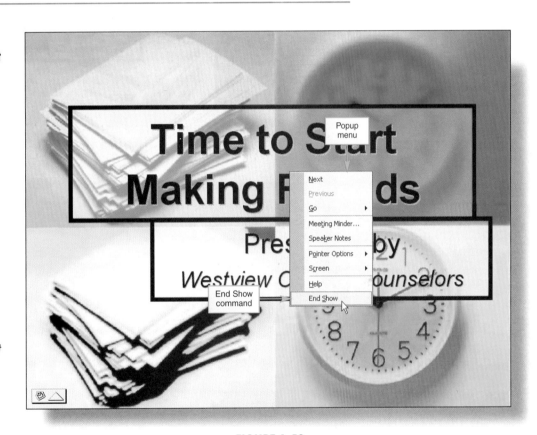

FIGURE 1-59

Quitting PowerPoint

The Make Friends presentation now is complete. When you quit PowerPoint, PowerPoint prompts you to save any changes made to the presentation since the last save, closes all PowerPoint windows, and then quits PowerPoint. Closing PowerPoint returns control to the desktop. Perform the steps on the next page to quit PowerPoint.

Other Ways

1. Click last slide in presentation (returns to normal view to slide at which slide show view began)
2. Press ESC (displays slide last viewed in slide show view)
3. In Voice Command mode say "Escape"

Steps **To Quit PowerPoint**

1 **Point to the Close button on the PowerPoint title bar (Figure 1-60).**

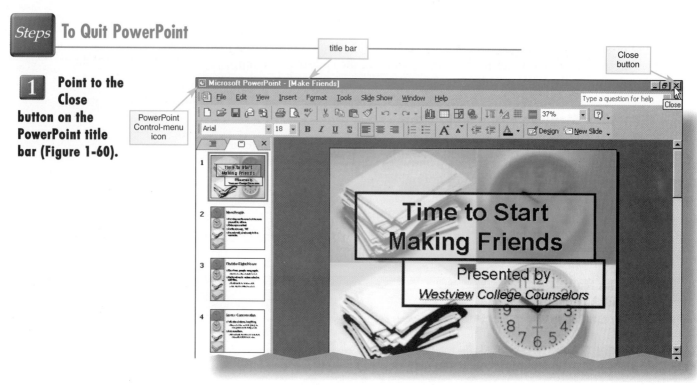

FIGURE 1-60

2 **Click the Close button.**

PowerPoint closes and the Windows desktop displays (Figure 1-61). If you made changes to the presentation since your last save, a Microsoft PowerPoint dialog box displays asking if you want to save changes. Clicking the Yes button saves the changes to the presentation before closing PowerPoint. Clicking the No button quits PowerPoint without saving the changes. Clicking the Cancel button returns to the presentation.

FIGURE 1-61

1. Double-click PowerPoint Control-menu icon; or click PowerPoint Control-menu icon, on Control menu click Close
2. On File menu click Exit
3. Press CTRL+Q or press ALT+F4

Opening a Presentation

Earlier, you saved the presentation on a floppy disk using the file name, Make Friends. Once you create and save a presentation, you may need to retrieve it from the floppy disk to make changes. For example, you may want to replace the design template or modify some text. Recall that a presentation is a PowerPoint document. Use the **Open Office Document command** to open an existing presentation.

Opening an Existing Presentation

Be sure that the floppy disk used to save the Make Friends presentation is in drive A. Then, perform the following steps to open the presentation using the Open Office Document command on the Start menu.

More About

Sound Files

Creating slide shows can be exciting if you add sound cues that play sounds when you scroll, open dialog boxes, and zoom in or out. You can download sound files from the Microsoft Web site. For more information, visit the PowerPoint 2002 More About Web page (scsite.com/ pp2002/more.htm) and then click Sound Files.

 To Open an Existing Presentation

1 **Click the Start button on the Windows taskbar and then point to Open Office Document.**

The Windows Start menu displays and Open Office Document is highlighted (Figure 1-62). The ScreenTip displays the function of the command.

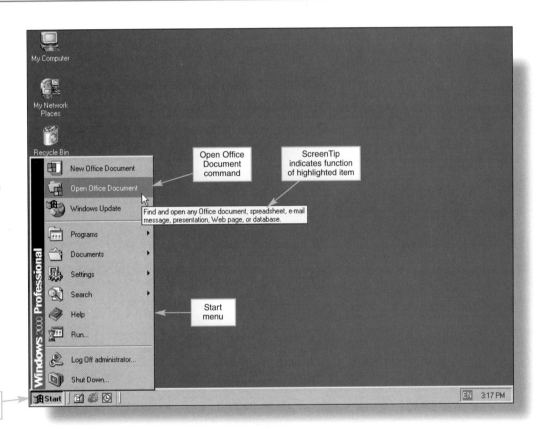

FIGURE 1-62

2 **Click Open Office Document. When the Open Office Document dialog box displays, if necessary, click the Look in box arrow and then click 3½ Floppy (A:) in the Look in list.**

The Open Office Document dialog box displays (Figure 1-63). A list of existing files displays on drive A. Notice that Office Files displays in the Files of type box. The file, Make Friends, is highlighted. Your list of existing files may be different depending on the files saved on your floppy disk.

FIGURE 1-63

3 **Double-click the file name, Make Friends.**

PowerPoint starts, opens Make Friends on drive A, and displays the first slide in the PowerPoint window (Figure 1-64). The presentation displays in normal view because PowerPoint opens a presentation in the same view in which it was saved.

FIGURE 1-64

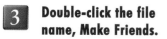

Other Ways

1. Click Open button on Standard toolbar, select file name, click Open button in Open Office Document dialog box
2. On File menu click Open, select file name, click Open button in Open dialog box
3. From desktop, right-click Start button, click either Open or Open All Users on shortcut menu, double-click Open Office Document, select file name, click Open button in Open Office Document dialog box
4. In Voice Command mode, say "Open file, [type file name], Open"

When you start PowerPoint and open Make Friends, the application name and file name display on a recessed button on the Windows taskbar. When more than one application is open, you can switch between applications by clicking the appropriate application button.

Checking a Presentation for Spelling and Consistency

After you create a presentation, you should check it visually for spelling errors and style consistency. In addition, you can use PowerPoint's Spelling and Style tools to identify possible misspellings and inconsistencies.

Checking a Presentation for Spelling Errors

PowerPoint checks the entire presentation for spelling mistakes using a standard dictionary contained in the Microsoft Office group. This dictionary is shared with the other Microsoft Office applications such as Word and Excel. A **custom dictionary** is available if you want to add special words such as proper names, cities, and acronyms. When checking a presentation for spelling errors, PowerPoint opens the standard dictionary and the custom dictionary file, if one exists. When a word displays in the Spelling dialog box, you perform one of the actions listed in Table 1-3.

More About

Spelling Checker

While PowerPoint's Spelling checker is a valuable tool, it is not infallible. You should proofread your presentation carefully by saying each word aloud and pointing to each word as you say it. Be mindful of commonly misused words such as its and it's, their and they're, and you're and your.

Table 1-3 Summary of Spelling Checker Actions

FEATURE	DESCRIPTION
Ignore the word	Click the Ignore button when the word is spelled correctly but not found in the dictionaries. PowerPoint continues checking the rest of the presentation.
Ignore all occurrences of the word	Click the Ignore All button when the word is spelled correctly but not found in the dictionaries. PowerPoint ignores all occurrences of the word and continues checking the rest of the presentation.
Select a different spelling	Click the proper spelling of the word from the list in the Suggestions box. Click the Change button. PowerPoint corrects the word and continues checking the rest of the presentation.
Change all occurrences of the misspelling to a different spelling	Click the proper spelling of the word from the list in the Suggestions box. Click the Change All button. PowerPoint changes all occurrences of the misspelled word and continues checking the rest of the presentation.
Add a word to the custom dictionary	Click the Add button. PowerPoint opens the custom dictionary, adds the word, and continues checking the rest of the presentation.
View alternative spellings	Click the Suggest button. PowerPoint lists suggested spellings. Click the correct word from the Suggestions box or type the proper spelling. Then click the Change button. PowerPoint continues checking the rest of the presentation.
Add spelling error to AutoCorrect list	Click the AutoCorrect button. PowerPoint adds the spelling error and its correction to the AutoCorrect list. Any future misspelling of the word is corrected automatically as you type.
Close	Click the Close button to close the Spelling checker and return to the PowerPoint window.

The standard dictionary contains commonly used English words. It does not, however, contain proper names, abbreviations, technical terms, poetic contractions, or antiquated terms. PowerPoint treats words not found in the dictionaries as misspellings.

Starting the Spelling Checker

Perform the steps on the next page to start the Spelling checker and check the entire presentation.

Steps **To Start the Spelling Checker**

1 Point to the Spelling button on the Standard toolbar (Figure 1-65).

FIGURE 1-65

2 Click the Spelling button. When the Spelling dialog box displays, point to the Ignore button.

PowerPoint starts the Spelling checker and displays the Spelling dialog box (Figure 1-66). The word, Westview, displays in the Not in Dictionary box. Depending on the custom dictionary, Westview may not be recognized as a misspelled word.

FIGURE 1-66

3 Click the Ignore button. When the Microsoft PowerPoint dialog box displays, point to the OK button.

PowerPoint ignores the word, Westview, and continues searching for additional misspelled words. PowerPoint may stop on additional words depending on your typing accuracy. When PowerPoint has checked all slides for misspellings, it displays the Microsoft PowerPoint dialog box informing you that the spelling check is complete (Figure 1-67).

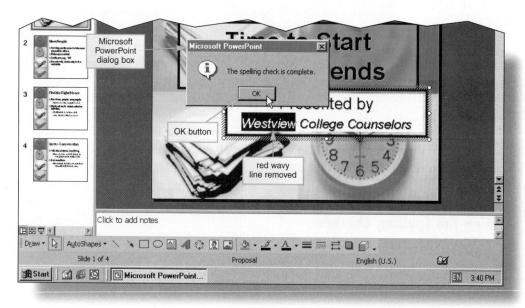

FIGURE 1-67

4 **Click the OK button.**

PowerPoint closes the Spelling checker and returns to the current slide, Slide 1 (Figure 1-68), or to the slide where a possible misspelled word displayed.

FIGURE 1-68

Other Ways

1. On Tools menu click Spelling
2. Press ALT+T, press S; when finished, press ENTER
3. In Voice Command mode, say "Tools, Spelling"

The red wavy line below the word, Westview, is gone because you instructed PowerPoint to ignore that word, which does not appear in the standard dictionary. You also could have added that word to the dictionary so it would not be flagged as a possible misspelled word in subsequent presentations you create using that word.

Correcting Errors

After creating a presentation and running the Spelling checker, you may find that you must make changes. Changes may be required because a slide contains an error, the scope of the presentation shifts, or the style is inconsistent. This section explains the types of errors that commonly occur when creating a presentation.

Types of Corrections Made to Presentations

You generally make three types of corrections to text in a presentation: additions, deletions, and replacements.

- **Additions** are necessary when you omit text from a slide and need to add it later. You may need to insert text in the form of a sentence, word, or single character. For example, you may want to add the rest of the presenter's first name on the title slide.
- **Deletions** are required when text on a slide is incorrect or no longer is relevant to the presentation. For example, a slide may look cluttered. Therefore, you may want to remove one of the bulleted paragraphs to add more space.
- **Replacements** are needed when you want to revise the text in a presentation. For example, you may want to substitute the word, their, for the word, there.

Editing text in PowerPoint basically is the same as editing text in a word processing package. The following sections illustrate the most common changes made to text in a presentation.

Quick Reference

For a table that lists how to complete tasks covered in this book using the mouse, menu, shortcut menu, and keyboard, see the Quick Reference Summary at the back of this book or visit the Shelly Cashman Series Office XP Web page (scsite.com/offxp/qr.htm) and then click Microsoft PowerPoint 2002.

Deleting Text

You can delete text using one of four methods. One is to use the BACKSPACE key to remove text just typed. The second is to position the insertion point to the left of the text you wish to delete and then press the DELETE key. The third method is to double-click the word you wish to delete and then type the correct text. The fourth method is to drag through the text you wish to delete and then press the DELETE key. (Use the fourth method when deleting large sections of text.)

Table 1-4	Appearance in Black and White View
OBJECT	**APPEARANCE IN BLACK AND WHITE VIEW**
Bitmaps	Grayscale
Embossing	Hidden
Fills	Grayscale
Frame	Black
Lines	Black
Object shadows	Grayscale
Pattern fills	Grayscale
Slide backgrounds	White
Text	Black
Text shadows	Hidden

Replacing Text in an Existing Slide

When you need to correct a word or phrase, you can replace the text by selecting the text to be replaced and then typing the new text. As soon as you press any key on the keyboard, the highlighted text is deleted and the new text displays.

PowerPoint inserts text to the left of the insertion point. The text to the right of the insertion point moves to the right (and shifts downward if necessary) to accommodate the added text.

Displaying a Presentation in Black and White

Printing handouts of a presentation allows you to use them to make overhead transparencies. The **Color/Grayscale button** on the Standard toolbar displays the presentation in black and white before you print. Table 1-4 identifies how PowerPoint objects display in black and white.

Perform the following steps to display the presentation in black and white.

Steps **To Display a Presentation in Black and White**

1 **Click the Color/ Grayscale button on the Standard toolbar and then point to Pure Black and White in the list.**

The Color/Grayscale list displays (Figure 1-69). Pure Black and White alters the slides' appearance so that only black lines display on a white background. Grayscale displays varying degrees of gray.

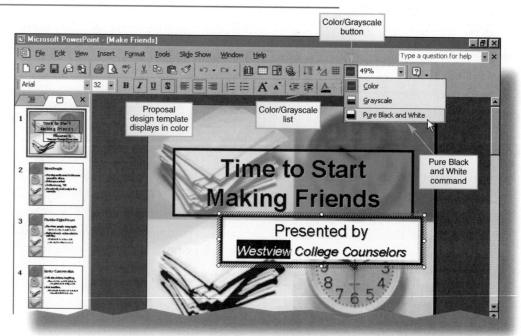

FIGURE 1-69

2 **Click Pure Black and White.**

Slide 1 displays in black and white in the slide pane (Figure 1-70). The four slide thumbnails display in color in the Slides tab. The Grayscale View toolbar displays. The Color/Grayscale button on the Standard toolbar changes from color bars to black and white.

FIGURE 1-70

3 **Click the Next Slide button three times to view all slides in the presentation in black and white. Point to the Close Black and White View button on the Grayscale View toolbar (Figure 1-71).**

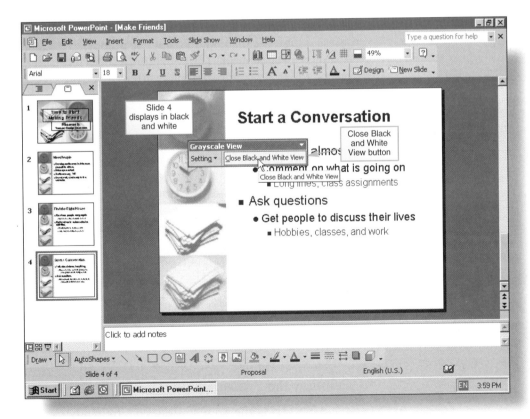

FIGURE 1-71

| **4** | **Click the Close Black and White View button.** |

Slide 4 displays with the default Proposal color scheme (Figure 1-72).

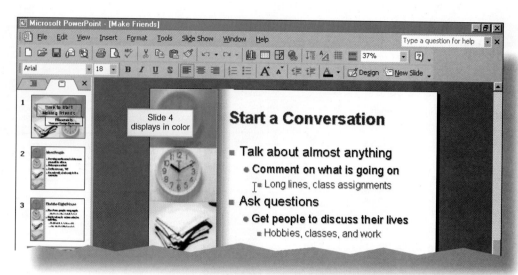

FIGURE 1-72

After you view the text objects in the presentation in black and white, you can make any changes that will enhance printouts produced from a black and white printer or photocopier.

Printing a Presentation

After you create a presentation, you often want to print it. A printed version of the presentation is called a **hard copy**, or **printout**. The first printing of the presentation is called a **rough draft**. The rough draft allows you to proofread the presentation to check for errors and readability. After correcting errors, you print the final copy of the presentation.

Saving Before Printing

Before printing a presentation, you should save your work in the event you experience difficulties with the printer. You occasionally may encounter system problems that can be resolved only by restarting the computer. In such an instance, you will need to reopen the presentation. As a precaution, always save the presentation before you print. Perform the following steps to save the presentation before printing.

TO SAVE A PRESENTATION BEFORE PRINTING

| **1** | Verify that the floppy disk is in drive A. |
| **2** | Click the Save button on the Standard toolbar. |

All changes made after your last save now are saved on a floppy disk.

Printing the Presentation

After saving the presentation, you are ready to print. Clicking the **Print button** on the Standard toolbar causes PowerPoint to print all slides in the presentation. Perform the following steps to print the presentation slides.

Steps To Print a Presentation

1 **Ready the printer according to the printer instructions. Then click the Print button on the Standard toolbar.**

The printer icon in the tray status area on the Windows taskbar indicates a print job is processing (Figure 1-73). After several moments, the slide show begins printing on the printer. When the presentation is finished printing, the printer icon in the tray status area on the Windows taskbar no longer displays.

2 **When the printer stops, retrieve the printouts of the slides.**

The presentation, Make Friends, prints on four pages (Figures 1-2a through 1-2d on page PP 1.09).

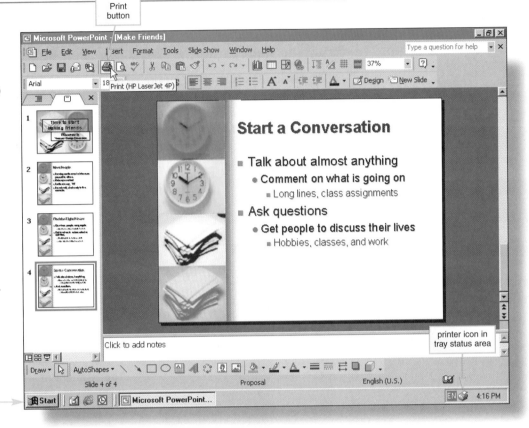

FIGURE 1-73

You can click the printer icon next to the clock in the tray status area on the Windows taskbar to obtain information about the presentations printing on your printer and to delete files in the print queue that are waiting to be printed.

Making a Transparency

With the handouts printed, you now can make overhead transparencies using one of several devices. One device is a printer attached to your computer, such as an ink-jet printer or a laser printer. Transparencies produced on a printer may be in black and white or color, depending on the printer. Another device is a photocopier. Because each of these devices requires a special transparency film, check the user's manual for the film requirement of your specific device, or ask your instructor.

PowerPoint Help System

You can get answers to PowerPoint questions at any time by using the **PowerPoint Help system**. Used properly, this form of assistance can increase your productivity and reduce your frustrations by minimizing the time you spend learning how to use PowerPoint.

Other Ways

1. On File menu click Print
2. Press CTRL+P or press CTRL+SHIFT+F12
3. In Voice Command mode, say "Print"

More About

The PowerPoint Help System

The best way to become familiar with the PowerPoint Help system is to use it. Appendix A includes detailed information on the PowerPoint Help system and exercises that will help you gain confidence in using it.

The following section shows how to get answers to your questions using the Ask a Question box on the menu bar. For additional information on using the PowerPoint Help system, see Appendix A and Table 1-5 on page PP 1.65.

Obtaining Help Using the Ask a Question Box on the Menu Bar

The **Ask a Question box** on the right side of the menu bar lets you type free-form questions such as, how do I save or how do I create a Web page, or you can type terms such as, copy, save, or format. PowerPoint responds by displaying a list of topics related to what you typed. The following steps show how to use the Ask a Question box to obtain information on formatting a presentation.

Steps **To Obtain Help Using the Ask a Question Box**

1 **Click the Ask a Question box on the right side of the menu bar and then type** bullet **(Figure 1-74).**

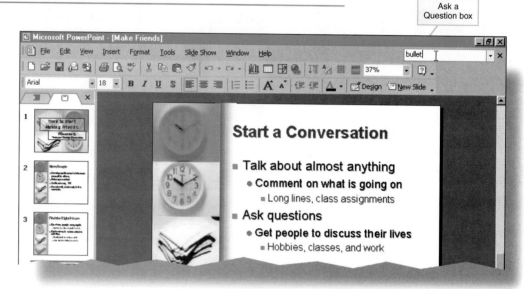

FIGURE 1-74

2 **Press the ENTER key. When the list of topics displays below the Ask a Question box, point to the topic, Change the bullet style in a list.**

A list of topics displays relating to the phrase, change the bullet style in a list (Figure 1-75). The mouse pointer changes to a hand, which indicates it is pointing to a link.

FIGURE 1-75

3 **Click Change the bullet style in a list. When the Microsoft PowerPoint Help window displays, double-click its title bar to maximize it. Point to Change the bullet style for a single list.**

A Microsoft PowerPoint Help window displays that provides Help information about changing the bullet style for a slide (Figure 1-76). The mouse pointer changes to a hand. The Index, Answer Wizard, or Content sheet is active on the left side of the Microsoft PowerPoint Help window.

FIGURE 1-76

4 **Click Change the bullet style for a single list. Point to Change the bullet color.**

Directions for changing a bullet style on a single slide display. Options include changing a bullet character, changing a bullet size, and changing a bullet color (Figure 1-77).

FIGURE 1-77

5 **Click Change the bullet color. Point to the Close button on the Microsoft PowerPoint Help window title bar.**

Specific details of changing the color of the bullets on a slide display (Figure 1-78).

6 **Click the Close button on the Microsoft PowerPoint Help window title bar.**

The PowerPoint Help window closes, and the PowerPoint presentation displays.

FIGURE 1-78

 Ways

1. Click Microsoft PowerPoint Help button on Standard toolbar; or on Help menu click Microsoft PowerPoint Help
2. Press F1

Use the buttons in the upper-left corner of the Microsoft PowerPoint Help window (Figure 1-76 on page PP 1.63) to navigate through the Help system, change the display, and print the contents of the window.

As you enter questions and terms in the Ask a Question box, PowerPoint adds them to its list. Thus, if you click the Ask a Question box arrow, a list of previously asked questions and terms will display.

Table 1-5 summarizes the 10 categories of Help available to you. Because of the way the PowerPoint Help system works, be certain to review the rightmost column of Table 1-5 if you have difficulties activating the desired category of help. For additional information on using the PowerPoint Help system, see Appendix A.

Quitting PowerPoint

Project 1 is complete. The final task is to close the presentation and quit PowerPoint. Perform the following steps to quit PowerPoint.

TO QUIT POWERPOINT

1 Click the Close button on the title bar.

2 If prompted to save the presentation before quitting PowerPoint, click the Yes button in the Microsoft PowerPoint dialog box.

Table 1-5　PowerPoint Help System

TYPE	DESCRIPTION	HOW TO ACTIVATE
Answer Wizard	Answers questions or searches for terms that you type in your own words.	Click the Microsoft PowerPoint Help button on the Standard toolbar. Click the Answer Wizard tab.
Ask a Question box	Answers questions or searches for terms that you type in your own words.	Type a question or term in the Ask a Question box on the menu bar and then press the ENTER key.
Contents sheet	Groups Help topics by general categories. Use when you know only the general category of the topic in question.	Click the Microsoft PowerPoint Help button on the Standard toolbar. Click the Contents tab.
Detect and Repair	Automatically finds and fixes errors in the application.	Click Detect and Repair on the Help menu.
Hardware and Software Information	Shows Product ID and allows access to system information and technical support information.	Click About Microsoft PowerPoint on the Help menu and then click the appropriate button.
Index sheet	Similar to an index in a book. Use when you know exactly what you want.	Click the Microsoft PowerPoint Help button on the Standard toolbar. If necessary, maximize the Help window by double-clicking its title bar. Click the Index tab.
Office Assistant	Similar to the Ask a Question box in that the Office Assistant answers questions that you type in your own words, offers tips, and provides help for a variety of PowerPoint features.	Click the Office Assistant icon if it is on the screen. If the Office Assistant does not display, click Show the Office Assistant on the Help menu.
Office on the Web	Used to access technical resources and download free product enhancements on the Web.	Click Office on the Web on the Help menu.
Question Mark button	Used to identify unfamiliar items in a dialog box.	Click the Question Mark button on the title bar of a dialog box and then click an item in the dialog box.
What's This? Command	Used to identify unfamiliar items on the screen.	Click What's This? on the Help menu, and then click an item on the screen.

C A S E　P E R S P E C T I V E　S U M M A R Y

Jennifer Williams is pleased with the Time to Start Making Friends PowerPoint slide show. The counseling staff will present methods of facing loneliness to incoming freshmen attending orientation sessions at your school. The four slides display a variety of ways students can make friends on campus. The title slide identifies the topic of the presentation, and the next three slides give key pointers regarding going to appropriate places to meet people and start a conversation. The counselors will use your slides to make overhead transparencies to organize their speeches, and the students will keep handouts of your slides for future reference.

Project Summary

Project 1 introduced you to starting PowerPoint and creating a presentation consisting of a title slide and single- and multi-level bulleted lists. You learned about PowerPoint design templates, objects, and attributes. This project illustrated how to create an interesting introduction to a presentation by changing the text font style to italic and increasing font size on the title slide. Completing these tasks, you saved the presentation. Then, you created three text slides with bulleted lists, two with multi-level bullets, to explain how to meet friends in college. Next, you learned how to view the presentation in slide show view. Then, you learned how to quit PowerPoint and how to open an existing presentation. You used the Spelling checker to search for spelling errors. You learned how to display the presentation in black and white. You learned how to print hard copies of the slides in order to make handouts and overhead transparencies. Finally, you learned how to use the PowerPoint Help system.

What You Should Know

Having completed this project, you now should be able to perform the following tasks:

- Add a New Slide and Enter a Slide Title *(PP 1.37)*
- Add a New Text Slide with a Bulleted List *(PP 1.32)*
- Change the Text Font Style to Italic *(PP 1.26)*
- Choose a Design Template *(PP 1.19)*
- Create a Third-Level Paragraph *(PP 1.41)*
- Create Slide 4 *(PP 1.41)*
- Customize the PowerPoint Window *(PP 1.12)*
- Display a Presentation in Black and White *(PP 1.58)*
- Display the Popup Menu and Go to a Specific Slide *(PP 1.50)*
- End a Slide Show with a Black Slide *(PP 1.44)*
- Enter a Slide Title *(PP 1.34)*
- Enter the Presentation Subtitle *(PP 1.24)*
- Enter the Presentation Title *(PP 1.22)*
- Increase Font Size *(PP 1.27)*
- Move Manually Through Slides in a Slide Show *(PP 1.49)*
- Obtain Help Using the Ask a Question Box *(PP 1.62)*
- Open an Existing Presentation *(PP 1.53)*
- Print a Presentation *(PP 1.61)*
- Quit PowerPoint *(PP 1.52, 1.64)*
- Save a Presentation Before Printing *(PP 1.60)*
- Save a Presentation on a Floppy Disk *(PP 1.29)*
- Save a Presentation with the Same File Name *(PP 1.45)*
- Select a Text Placeholder *(PP 1.34)*
- Start PowerPoint *(PP 1.10)*
- Start Slide Show View *(PP 1.48)*
- Start the Spelling Checker *(PP 1.56)*
- Type a Multi-Level Bulleted List *(PP 1.38)*
- Type a Single-Level Bulleted List *(PP 1.35)*
- Type the Remaining Text for Slide 3 *(PP 1.40)*
- Type the Remaining Text for Slide 4 *(PP 1.43)*
- Use the Popup Menu to End a Slide Show *(PP 1.51)*
- Use the Scroll Box on the Slide Pane to Move to Another Slide *(PP 1.46)*

More About

Microsoft Certification

The Microsoft Office User Specialist (MOUS) Certification program provides an opportunity for you to obtain a valuable industry credential — proof that you have the PowerPoint 2002 skills required by employers. For more information, see Appendix E or visit the Shelly Cashman Series MOUS Web page at scsite.com/offxp/cert.htm.

Learn It Online

Instructions: To complete the Learn It Online excercises, start your browser, click the Address bar, and then enter scsite.com/offxp/exs.htm. When the Office XP Learn It Online page displays, follow the instructions in the exercises below.

1 Project Reinforcement TF, MC, and SA

Below PowerPoint Project 1, click the Project Reinforcement link. Print the quiz by clicking Print on the File menu. Answer each question. Write your first and last name at the top of each page, and then hand in the printout to your instructor.

2 Flash Cards

Below PowerPoint Project 1, click the Flash Cards link. When Flash Cards displays, read the instructions. Type 20 (or a number specified by your instructor) in the Number of Playing Cards text box, type your name in the Name text box, and then click the Flip Card button. When the flash card displays, read the question and then click the Answer box arrow to select an answer. Flip through Flash Cards. Click Print on the File menu to print the last flash card if your score is 15 (75%) correct or greater and then hand it in to your instructor. If your score is less than 15 (75%) correct, then redo this exercise by clicking the Replay button.

3 Practice Test

Below PowerPoint Project 1, click the Practice Test link. Answer each question, enter your first and last name at the bottom of the page, and then click the Grade Test button. When the graded practice test displays on your screen, click Print on the File menu to print a hard copy. Continue to take practice tests until you score 80% or better. Hand in a printout of the final practice test to your instructor.

4 Who Wants to Be a Computer Genius?

Below PowerPoint Project 1, click the Computer Genius link. Read the instructions, enter your first and last name at the bottom of the page, and then click the Play button. Hand in your score to your instructor.

5 Wheel of Terms

Below PowerPoint Project 1, click the Wheel of Terms link. Read the instructions, and then enter your first and last name and your school name. Click the Play button. Hand in your score.

6 Crossword Puzzle Challenge

Below PowerPoint Project 1, click the Crossword Puzzle Challenge link. Read the instructions, and then enter your first and last name. Click the Play button. Work the crossword puzzle. When you are finished, click the Submit button. When the crossword puzzle redisplays, click the Print button. Hand in the printout.

7 Tips and Tricks

Below PowerPoint Project 1, click the Tips and Tricks link. Click a topic that pertains to Project 1. Right-click the information and then click Print on the shortcut menu. Construct a brief example of what the information relates to in PowerPoint to confirm you understand how to use the tip or trick. Hand in the example and printed information.

8 Newsgroups

Below PowerPoint Project 1, click the Newsgroups link. Click a topic that pertains to Project 1. Print three comments. Hand in the comments.

9 Expanding Your Horizons

Below PowerPoint Project 1, click the Articles for Microsoft PowerPoint link. Click a topic that pertains to Project 1. Print the information. Construct a brief example of what the information relates to in PowerPoint to confirm you understand the contents of the article. Hand in the example and printed information.

10 Search Sleuth

Below PowerPoint Project 1, click the Search Sleuth link. To search for a term that pertains to this project, select a term below the Project 1 title and then use the Google search engine at google.com (or any major search engine) to display and print two Web pages that present information on the term. Hand in the printout.

Apply Your Knowledge

1 Trends in Computer Technology

Instructions: Start PowerPoint. Open the presentation Computer Trends from the Data Disk. See the inside back cover of this book for instructions for downloading the Data Disk or see your instructor for information on accessing the files required for this book. This slide lists hardware and software trends in the computer industry. Perform the following tasks to change the slide so it looks like the one in Figure 1-79.

1. Click the Slide Design button on the Formatting toolbar. Scroll down and then choose the Kimono design template (row 12, column 1).

2. Select the title text. Click the Italic button on the Formatting toolbar.

3. Click the Font Size box arrow on the Font Size button on the Formatting toolbar and then click font size 36.

4. Click the paragraph, Microdisplays the size of stamps. Click the Increase Indent button on the Formatting toolbar to change the paragraph to a second-level paragraph. Then change these three paragraphs to second-level paragraphs: Digital books, Speech recognition, and Control of home systems.

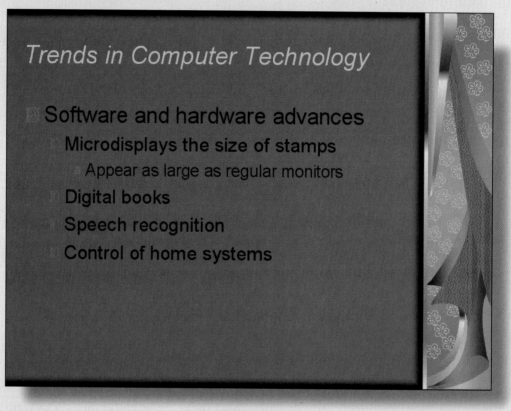

FIGURE 1-79

5. Click the Appear as large as regular monitors paragraph. Click the Increase Indent button on the Formatting toolbar twice to change this paragraph to a third-level paragraph.

6. Click File on the menu bar and then click Save As. Type Trends in Technology in the File name text box. If drive A is not already displaying in the Save in box, click the Save in box arrow, and then click 3½ Floppy (A:). Click the Save button.

7. Click the Color/Grayscale button on the Standard toolbar, and then click Pure Black and White to display the presentation in black and white.

8. Click the Print button on the Standard toolbar.

9. Click the Close Black and White View button on the Grayscale View toolbar.

10. Click the Close button on the title bar to quit PowerPoint.

11. Write your name on the printout, and hand it in to your instructor.

In the Lab

Note: These labs require you to create presentations based on notes. When you design these slide shows, use the 7 × 7 rule, which states that each line should have a maximum of seven words, and each slide should have a maximum of seven lines.

1 Decades of Nutrition in the Twentieth Century

Problem: You are enrolled in a health class, and one of your assignments is to analyze nutrition and eating habits during the twentieth century. You decide to prepare a presentation for your class discussing food and related health problems during 20-year periods. You first develop the notes shown in Figure 1-80, and then you create the presentation shown in Figures 1-81a through 1-81f on pages PP 1.70 and PP 1.71.

I) Decades of Nutrition
Eating in the Twentieth Century
  A) Presented by
  B) Melissa Ruiz
  C) Health 101
II) 1900 - 1919
  A) Cold breakfast cereals introduced
  B) Ice cream sales soar
    1) First ice cream cone served
  C) Hershey introduces its chocolate bar
  D) Plump is preferred body type
    1) Slim is considered sickly
III) 1920 – 1939
  A) Kraft introduces Macaroni and Cheese
    1) Cooking from scratch begins to decline
  B) Red meat, vegetable intakes increase
  C) Heart disease on the rise
    1) Surpasses TB as leading cause of death
  D) Slim becomes preferred body type
IV) 1940 - 1959
  A) First McDonald's Hamburgers opens
    1) Home cooking begins to decline
  B) Research links heart disease with high saturated fats
  C) Fewer than 25 percent of Americans have healthy diets
V) 1960 - 1979
  A) Whole grains, Vitamin C gain popularity
  B) Soft drink consumption increases
    1) Exceeds milk consumption by 1980
  C) Federal committee finds unhealthy diets
    1) Too high in fats, sugar, salt, and meat
    2) Too low in grains, fruits, and vegetables
VI) 1980 - 1999
  A) Low-fat snacks flood grocery stores
    1) Americans still become more overweight
  B) Omega-3 fats found heart-healthy
    1) Found in fish, flaxseed
  C) Fish consumption increases
  D) Dairy and egg intakes decrease

FIGURE 1-80

In the Lab

Decades of Nutrition in the Twentieth Century *(continued)*

Decades of Nutrition

Eating in the Twentieth Century

Presented by
Melissa Ruiz
Health 101

(a) Slide 1 (Title Slide)

1900 - 1919

- Cold breakfast cereals introduced
- Ice cream sales soar
  - First ice cream cone served
- Hershey introduces its chocolate bar
- Plump is preferred body type
  - Slim is considered sickly

(b) Slide 2

1920 – 1939

- Kraft introduces Macaroni and Cheese
  - Cooking from scratch begins to decline
- Red meat, vegetable intakes increase
- Heart disease on the rise
  - Surpasses TB as leading cause of death
- Slim becomes preferred body type

(c) Slide 3

1940 - 1959

- First McDonald's Hamburgers opens
  - Home cooking begins to decline
- Research links heart disease with high saturated fats
  - Fewer than 25 percent of Americans have healthy diets

(d) Slide 4

FIGURE 1-81

In the Lab

1960 - 1979

➢ Whole grains, Vitamin C gain popularity
➢ Soft drink consumption increases
  • Exceeds milk consumption by 1980
➢ Federal committee finds unhealthy diets
  • Too high in fats, sugar, salt, and meat
  • Too low in grains, fruits, and vegetables

(e) Slide 5

1980 - 1999

➢ Low-fat snacks flood grocery stores
  • Americans still become more overweight
➢ Omega-3 fats found heart-healthy
  • Found in fish, flaxseed
    - Fish consumption increases
➢ Dairy and egg intakes decrease

(f) Slide 6

FIGURE 1-81 *(continued)*

Instructions: Perform the following tasks.

1. Create a new presentation using the Ripple design template (row 19, column 1).
2. Using the typed notes illustrated in Figure 1-80, create the title slide shown in Figure 1-81a using your name in place of Melissa Ruiz. Italicize your name. Decrease the font size of the second paragraph of the title text to 36. Decrease the font size of the paragraph, Presented by, to 28. Decrease the font size of the paragraph, Health 101, to 24.
3. Using the typed notes in Figure 1-80 on page PP 1.69, create the five text slides with bulleted lists shown in Figures 1-81b through 1-81f.
4. Click the Spelling button on the Standard toolbar. Correct any errors.
5. Save the presentation using the file name, Nutrition.
6. Display the presentation in black and white.
7. Print the black and white presentation. Quit PowerPoint.

(continued)

In the Lab

2 Select Electric Products Open House

Problem: You work at Select Electric, a local store featuring a variety of electronic products. Your manager has asked you to participate in the semi-annual open house showcasing the latest consumer electronics. You decide to get involved by developing a PowerPoint presentation that helps customers view key features of various devices. You review the products that will be featured and develop the list shown in Figure 1-82. Then, you select a PowerPoint design template and decide to modify it.

I) Electronics Explosion
  A) Presented by
  B) Select Electric
II) High-Definition TV
  A) Screens from 34 to 61 inches
  B) Some models have two tuners
      1) Picture-in-picture
        a) Watch two shows at once
  C) Inputs maximize digital sources
      1) DVD and satellite
III) Digital Camcorders
  A) Razor-sharp recording
      1) Image stabilization
  B) Crystal-clear audio
  C) Digital still photos
      1) Store on removable memory card
        a) CompactFlash, Memory Stick
IV) Digital Cameras
  A) Megapixels increase clarity
      1) 4.3, 3.3, 2.1 megapixels
  B) Optical and digital zoom
  C) MPEG movie mode
      1) Up to 60 seconds
        a) 15 frames per second

FIGURE 1-82

In the Lab

Instructions: Perform the following tasks.

1. Create a new presentation using the Fireworks design template (row 10, column 2).
2. Using the notes in Figure 1-82, create the title slide shown in Figure 1-83a. Increase the font size of the paragraph, Electronics Explosion, to 48 and change the text font style to italic. Decrease the font size of the paragraph, Presented by, to 28.
3. Using the notes in Figure 1-82, create the three text slides with multi-level bulleted lists shown in Figures 1-83b through 1-83d.

(a) Slide 1 (Title Slide)

(b) Slide 2

(c) Slide 3

(d) Slide 4

FIGURE 1-83

(continued)

In the Lab

Select Electric Products Open House *(continued)*

4. Click the Spelling button on the Standard toolbar. Correct any errors.
5. Drag the scroll box to display Slide 1. Click the Slide Show button to start slide show view. Then click to display each slide.
6. Save the presentation using the file name, Select Electric. Display and print the presentation in black and white. Quit PowerPoint.

3 West Shore College Job Fair

Problem: Your school, West Shore College, is planning a job fair to occur during the week of midterm exams. The Placement Office has invited 150 companies and local businesses to promote its current and anticipated job openings. The Placement Office director, Bob Thornton, hands you the outline shown in Figure 1-84 and asks you to prepare a presentation and handouts to promote the event.

Instructions: Using the list in Figure 1-84, design and create a presentation. The presentation must include a title slide and three text slides with bulleted lists. Perform the following tasks.

1. Create a new presentation using the Cliff design template (row 4, column 1).
2. Create a title slide titled, West Shore College Career Fair. Include a subtitle, using your name in place of Bob Thornton. Decrease the font size for paragraphs, Presented by, and, West Shore Placement Office, to 28. Italicize your name.
3. Using Figure 1-84 create three text slides with multi-level bulleted lists. On Slide 4, change the color of the diamond bullets from gold to white.
4. View the presentation in slide show view to look for errors. Correct any errors.
5. Check the presentation for spelling errors.
6. Save the presentation with the file name, Career Fair. Print the presentation slides in black and white. Quit PowerPoint.

In the Lab

I) West Shore College Career Fair
  A) Presented by
  B) West Shore Placement Office
  C) Bob Thornton, Director
II) Who Is Coming?
  A) National corporations
       1) Progressive companies looking for high-quality candidates
  B) Local companies
       1) Full-time and part-time
        a) Hundreds of jobs
III) When Is It?
  A) Midterm week
       1) Monday through Friday
  B) West Shore College Cafeteria
  C) Convenient hours
       1) 9:00 a.m. to 8:00 p.m.
IV) How Should I Prepare?
  A) Bring plenty of resumes
       1) More than 150 companies expected
  B) Dress neatly
  C) View the Placement Office Web site
       1) Up-to-date information
       2) Company profiles

FIGURE 1-84

Cases and Places

The difficulty of these case studies varies:
▌ are the least difficult; ▌▌ are more difficult; and ▌▌▌ are the most difficult.

Note: Remember to use the 7 × 7 rule as you design the presentations: a maximum of seven words on a line and a maximum of seven lines on one slide.

1 ▌ Fitness Center employees present many classes on a variety of physical and emotional wellness topics. The coordinator, Carol O'Malley, has contacted you to help her prepare a presentation that will be delivered at community fairs and at the local shopping mall. She has prepared the notes shown in Figure 1-85 and has asked you to use them to develop a title slide and additional text slides that can be used on an overhead projector. Use the concepts and techniques introduced in this project to create the presentation.

**Enhance Your Physical and Emotional Wellness
At the Mid-City College Fitness Center**
Carol O'Malley, director

Mind/Body Programs
Meditation
    Various techniques
    Time to practice included
Stress Management Workshop
    Relaxation strategies
    Four-part series

Lifestyle Programs
CPR and First Aid
    Certification and recertification
    American Red Cross instructors
Smoking Cessation
    Eight-session group program
    Individual consultations

Nutrition Programs
Nutrition Connection
    Semester-long program
    Change your lifestyle to enhance your health
    Achieve your weight-management goals
    Increase your self-esteem
Dining Out: Eat and Be Healthy

FIGURE 1-85

Cases and Places

2 ▶ More than 76 million Americans currently carry cellular telephones, and many of these people use their telephones while driving. Although 87 percent of adults believe using a cellular telephone impairs their ability to drive, motorists continue to place and receive calls while driving. Andy Allman, your Lo-Rate Insurance agent, knows you are learning PowerPoint and asks you to help him prepare a presentation that will be delivered at shopping centers and on campus. He has prepared the notes shown in Figure 1-86 and wants you to use them to develop a title slide and additional text slides for a presentation and handouts. Use the concepts and techniques introduced in this project to create the slide show.

Calling All Cars
Using Your Telephone Safely in Your Vehicle
Andy Allman
Lo-Rate Insurance Agency

Cellular telephones distract from driving
    37 percent of drivers say they have had a near miss with someone using a cellular telephone
    2 percent of drivers have had an accident with someone using a cellular telephone
    Some communities have banned cellular telephone use behind the wheel

Your telephone can be a safety tool
    More than 118,000 calls placed daily to 911 from cellular telephones
    Emergency response times have decreased as 911 calls have increased

Use your telephone responsibly
    Place calls before pulling into traffic
    Use your telephone's special features such as speed dial and redial
    Do not call in hazardous weather or heavy traffic
    Do not take notes or look up numbers while driving
    Do not engage in emotional or stressful conversations
    50 percent of drivers seldom or never use a telephone while driving

FIGURE 1-86

Cases and Places

3 ▶▶ Road Warrior is a business near campus that specializes in quick oil changes, headlight and windshield wiper replacement, flat repair, battery recharging, and interior and exterior cleaning. The owners, Homer and Hank Wilson, want to attract new customers, and they have asked you to help design a PowerPoint advertising campaign for them. Having graduated from your college, they are familiar with the vehicles students drive and the students' financial situations. Students can make appointments to bring their vehicles to the shop or to arrange for on-site service 24 hours a day. Road Warrior also carries a complete line of accessories, including lightbulbs, fuses, air fresheners, and air and oil filters. Many students consult with the technicians to plan for future service and to arrange financing for their repairs. The business is located in Highwood Mall, 1580 North Western Street, West Grove, Michigan. The telephone number is 555-2297. Using the techniques presented in this project, prepare a title slide and four text slides with bulleted lists for the presentation and for handouts.

4 ▶▶ Every year people suffer from more than one billion colds. While no remedy cures the runny nose and sore throat that accompany the common cold, students can reduce their chances of catching a cold and feel better when they are sick. Peter Script, the pharmacist at the drug store near campus, would like you to prepare a short PowerPoint presentation and handouts to educate customers about how to thwart the common cold. He tells you that students should get plenty of rest, drink plenty of fluids, and consume chicken soup when they feel cold symptoms. If their throats are sore, they should gargle with warm salt water or let a lozenge with menthol and a mild anesthetic dissolve slowly in their mouths. Decongestants help relieve a stuffy nose by shrinking blood vessels, but these drugs should not be taken for more than three days. Antihistamines relieve a runny nose, itching, and sneezing by having a drying effect. To avoid a cold, students should stay away from other people with colds, wash their hands frequently and keep them away from their mouths and noses, and dispose of tissues promptly. Using the techniques presented in this project, prepare a title slide and several text slides for their presentation and for handouts.

5 ▶▶ Family reunions are popular ways to unite relatives from all parts of the globe. You have successfully planned three reunions for your family, and your friends have asked you for assistance with their plans. You decide to prepare a PowerPoint presentation to share with them and use as a planning outline. As you reflect on your reunion successes, you recall that the first step is to find the right location for the event. You try to choose somewhere centrally located. You consider a city that everyone can reach by plane or by driving in a few hours, that has adequate accommodations, and a variety of tourist attractions for entertainment, sightseeing, and dining. Avoid cities with adverse weather conditions or with poor airline connections. Favorable cities are Dallas; Washington, D.C.; Las Vegas; and Reno/Lake Tahoe. Cruises and all-inclusive resorts are possibilities. Other planning tips are to use e-mail extensively to send plans to family members simultaneously and to use the Internet to find inexpensive airline tickets and explore the destination's Web site. Using the concepts and techniques presented in this project, prepare a title slide and at least three text slides for the presentation and for handouts.

Cases and Places

6 ▶▶▶ As discussed in the beginning of this project, approximately one-third of college students participate in student activities other than sports. Visit your campus student activities or Student Government
offices and discover what activities are among the more popular at school. Find out which events drew
the largest audiences this past semester, how much revenue was generated from these events, and what
the expenses were for the college. Then, learn which activities are planned for the next semester and for
next year. Who plans these events, and how are these individuals appointed or elected to these positions?
Using the concepts and techniques presented in this project, prepare a presentation to inform students
and staff about campus activities. Create a title slide and at least three additional slides that can be used
with an overhead projector and as handouts.

7 ▶▶▶ Dry cleaning expenses can affect a student's budget. Visit two local dry cleaning establishments and
obtain the costs of cleaning and pressing a shirt, a pair of pants, a jacket, and a dress. Discover if dis-
counts are available for students and on certain days of the week. Finally, learn how students may
reduce cleaning expenses by treating spots on their clothing. Then, using the concepts and techniques
presented in this project, prepare a presentation to report your findings. Create a title slide and at least
three additional slides that can be used with an overhead projector and as handouts.

Microsoft PowerPoint 2002

PROJECT

2

Using the Outline Tab and Clip Art to Create a Slide Show

You will have mastered the material in this project when you can:

O B J E C T I V E S

- Create a presentation from an outline
- Start and customize a new slide show
- Create a presentation using the Outline tab
- Add a slide on the Outline tab
- Create text slides with a single-level bulleted list on the Outline tab
- Create text slides with a multi-level bulleted list on the Outline tab
- Create a closing slide on the Outline tab
- Save and review a presentation
- Change the slide layout
- Insert clip art from the Microsoft Clip Organizer
- Use the Automatic Layout Options button
- Move clip art
- Change clip art size
- Add a header and footer to outline pages
- Add an animation scheme to a slide show
- Animate clip art
- Run an animated slide show
- Print a presentation outline
- E-mail a slide show from within PowerPoint

Plan, Prepare, and Practice

Formula for a Flawless Presentation

Public speaking are two words that strike panic in the hearts of millions of people the world over. The mere thought of standing in front of an audience and trying to maintain composure and focus to convey a message tops the list of absolute fears for the vast majority of people. When asked to describe their experience of public speaking, many individuals recall dry mouths, sweaty palms, queasy stomachs, and shaky knees.

Business News Now

- Sales have increased by an amazing 34%
- Employee productivity is up by 12%
- You just impressed your boss with a great presentation.

Now, with the powerful presentation graphics capabilities of PowerPoint, the anxiety of speech-making can be somewhat eased. You have learned that this software helps you organize your thoughts and present information in an orderly, attractive manner. In this project, you will add to your current knowledge of PowerPoint by creating a presentation from an outline, changing the slide layout, and inserting and modifying clip art from the Microsoft Clip Organizer. With the abundant tools available in PowerPoint, your slide shows will have visual appeal and ample content.

While the PowerPoint slide shows help you plan your speeches, they also help your audience absorb your message. People learn most effectively when their five senses are involved. Researchers have determined that individuals remember 10 percent of what they read, 20 percent of what they hear, 30 percent of what they see, and an amazing 70 percent when they both see and hear. That is why it is important to attend class instead of copying your classmate's notes. When you see and hear your instructor deliver a lecture and write your own notes, you are apt to interpret the concepts correctly and recall this information at the ever-important final exam.

The synergy of the speech-graphics combo is recognized in a variety of venues. For example, some college administrators and instructors are requiring students to register for their communications and PowerPoint classes concurrently. The theories of structuring effective communication presentations are deep rooted. Dale Carnegie wrote *How to Win Friends and Influence People* in 1936, and the millions of people who have read that book have learned practical advice on achieving success through communication. He formed the Dale Carnegie Institute, which has taught millions of graduates worldwide the techniques of sharing ideas effectively and persuading others. Microsoft has included Carnegie's four-step process — plan, prepare, practice, and present — in the PowerPoint Help system. Dale Carnegie Training® has incorporated Microsoft PowerPoint to provide powerful presentation tips in its courses and seminars.

In the days prior to PowerPoint, slides and overhead transparencies were the domain of artists in a corporation's graphic communications department. With the influx of Microsoft Office on desktops throughout a company, however, employees from all departments now develop the slide shows.

With proper planning, preparation, practice, and the popularity of PowerPoint for organizing ideas into artful presentations, speakers today successfully deliver their messages with poise and confidence.

Microsoft PowerPoint 2002

Using the Outline Tab and Clip Art to Create a Slide Show

CASE PERSPECTIVE

Cruising has taken on a new meaning for college students. Instead of driving endlessly with a few friends in an old car down boring neighborhood streets, today's students sail endlessly with friends on spectacular ships to exciting destinations. They experience an adventure they will never forget as they snorkel in crystal clear waters among glimmering tropical fish, explore fascinating cities, and watch the sun set from some of the most scenic locations in the world.

Wanting to capitalize on this vacation trend, the Office of Student Activities (OSA) at your school wants to sponsor a college-wide Spring Break cruise to the Caribbean. The Student Activities director, Maria Lopez, has asked you to help with the marketing efforts. She knows you have extensive computer experience and wants you to develop a PowerPoint presentation that advertises the trip and its highlights. The slide show will give an overview of the ports of call, activities, and cruise details. You decide to add clip art and animation to increase visual interest. Then you e-mail the completed presentation to Maria.

Introduction

At some time during either your academic or business life, you probably will make a presentation. The presentation may be informative by providing detailed information about a specific topic. Other presentations may be persuasive by selling a proposal or a product to a client, convincing management to approve a new project, or influencing the board of directors to accept the new fiscal budget. As an alternative to creating your presentation in the slide pane in normal view, as you did in Project 1, PowerPoint provides an outlining feature to help you organize your thoughts. When the outline is complete, it becomes the foundation for your presentation.

Project Two — Enjoy Spring Break in the Caribbean

Project 2 uses PowerPoint to create the five-slide Spring Break presentation shown in Figures 2-1a through 2-1e. You create the presentation from the outline shown in Figure 2-2 on page 2.06.

You can create your presentation outline using the Outline tab. When you create an outline, you type all the text at one time, as if you were typing an outline on a sheet of paper. This technique differs from creating a presentation in the slide pane in normal view, where you type text as you create each individual slide and the text displays in both the slide pane and on the Outline tab. PowerPoint creates the presentation as you type the outline by evaluating the outline structure and displaying a miniature view of the slide. Regardless of how you build a presentation, PowerPoint automatically creates the three views discussed in Project 1: normal, slide sorter, and slide show.

(a) Slide 1

(b) Slide 2

(c) Slide 3

(d) Slide 4

(e) Slide 5

FIGURE 2-1

The first step in creating a presentation on the Outline tab is to type a title for the outline. The **outline title** is the subject of the presentation and later becomes the presentation title text. Then, you type the remainder of the outline, indenting appropriately to establish a structure, or hierarchy. Once the outline is complete, you make your presentation more persuasive by adding **clips**, which are media files of art, animation, sound, and movies. This project uses outlining to create the presentation and clip art to support the text visually.

<table>
<tr><td>

I. Enjoy Spring Break in the Caribbean
  A. Warm Days, Cool Activities
  B. Sponsored by
  C. The Office of Student Activities
II. Onshore Adventures
  A. Golf, play volleyball, swim, and relax
  B. Experience a submarine tour
  C. Try parasailing
  D. Explore a rainforest
III. Onboard Activities
  A. Theaters, fitness center, and stores
    1. Make new friends
    2. Dance to the hits
  B. Indoor and outdoor pools and whirlpools
IV. Cruise Details
  A. Only $999, including all meals
    1. Seven-day vacation departs from Miami
  B. Unforgettable ports of call
    1. Frederiksted, St. Croix
    2. San Juan, Puerto Rico
    3. Charlotte Amalie, St. Thomas
V. Sign-Up Information
  A. Contact OSA
    1. Memorial Union
    2. Room 3110
    3. 9:00 a.m. to 5:00 p.m. daily
  B. Attend Caribbean Cruise Reception
    1. Office of Student Activities
    2. Friday, October 10
    3. 3:00 p.m. to 5:00 p.m.

</td></tr>
</table>

FIGURE 2-2

> ## More About
>
> ### The PowerPoint Help System
>
> Need Help? It is no further than the Ask a Question box in the upper-right corner of the window. Click the box that contains the text, Type a question for help (Figure 2-3), type `help`, and then press the ENTER key. PowerPoint will respond with a list of items you can click to learn about obtaining help on any PowerPoint-related topic. To find out what is new in PowerPoint 2002, type `what's new in PowerPoint` in the Ask a Question box.

Start a New Presentation

Project 1 introduced you to starting a presentation document, choosing a layout, and applying a design template. The following steps summarize how to start a new presentation, choose a layout, and apply a design template. To reset your toolbars and menus so they display exactly as shown in this book, follow the steps outlined in Appendix D. Perform the following steps to start and customize a new presentation.

TO START AND CUSTOMIZE A NEW PRESENTATION

1 Click the Start button on the Windows taskbar, point to Programs on the Start menu, and then click Microsoft PowerPoint on the Programs submenu.

2 If the New Presentation task pane displays, click the Show at startup check box to remove the check mark and then click the Close button on the task pane title bar.

3 If the Language bar displays, click its Minimize button.

4 Click the Slide Design button on the Formatting toolbar. When the Slide Design task pane displays, click the down scroll arrow in the Apply a design template list, and then click the Ocean template in the Available For Use area.

5 Click the Close button in the Slide Design task pane.

6 If the Standard and Formatting toolbars display on one row, click the Toolbar Options button on the right side of either toolbar and then click Show Buttons on Two Rows on the Toolbar Options menu.

PowerPoint displays the Title Slide layout and the Ocean template on Slide 1 in normal view (Figure 2-3).

title slide

Slide 1 of 1

view buttons

Normal View button selected

Ocean design template

FIGURE 2-3

Using the Outline Tab

The **Outline tab** provides a quick, easy way to create a presentation. **Outlining** allows you to organize your thoughts in a structured format. An outline uses indentation to establish a **hierarchy**, which denotes levels of importance to the main topic. An outline is a summary of thoughts, presented as headings and subheadings, often used as a preliminary draft when you create a presentation.

The three panes — tabs, slide, and notes — shown in normal view also display when you click the Outline tab. The notes pane displays below the slide pane. In the tabs pane, the slide text displays along with a slide number and a slide icon. Body text is indented below the title text. Objects, such as pictures, graphs, or tables, do not display. The slide icon is blank when a slide does not contain objects. The attributes for text on the Outline tab are the same as in normal view except for color and paragraph style.

PowerPoint formats a title style and five levels of body text in an outline. The outline begins with the slide title, which is not indented. The title is the main topic of the slide. Body text supporting the main topic begins on the first level and also is not indented. If desired, additional supporting text can be added on the second through

More *About*

Text Levels

While PowerPoint gives you five levels of body text to use on each slide, graphic designers suggest you limit your levels to three. The details on all five levels may overwhelm audiences. If you find yourself needing more than three levels, consider combining content in one level or using two different slides.

fifth levels. Each level is indented. Levels four and five generally are used for very detailed scientific and engineering presentations. Business and sales presentations usually focus on summary information and use the first, second, and third levels.

PowerPoint initially displays in normal view when you start a new presentation. To type the outline, click the Outline tab in the tabs pane. Perform the following steps to change to the Outline tab and display the Outlining toolbar.

Steps **To Change to the Outline Tab and Display the Outlining Toolbar**

1 **Point to the Outline tab located in the tabs pane.**

The tabs pane consists of the Outline tab and the Slides tab (Figure 2-4).

FIGURE 2-4

2 **Click the Outline tab.**

The Outline tab is selected. The tabs pane increases and the slide pane decreases in size.

3 **Click View on the menu bar and then point to Toolbars. Point to Outlining on the Toolbars submenu.**

The View menu and Toolbars submenu display (Figure 2-5).

FIGURE 2-5

4 **Click Outlining.**

The Outlining toolbar displays (Figure 2-6).

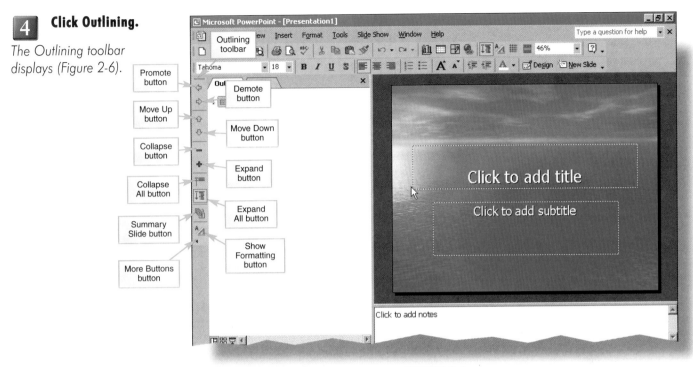

FIGURE 2-6

You can create and edit your presentation on the Outline tab. This tab also makes it easy to sequence slides and to relocate title text and body text from one slide to another. In addition to typing text to create a new presentation on the Outline tab, PowerPoint can produce slides from an outline created in Microsoft Word or another word processing application, if you save the outline as an RTF file or as a plain text file. The file extension **RTF** stands for **R**ich **T**ext **F**ormat.

Table 2-1 describes the buttons on the Outlining toolbar.

Table 2-1	**Buttons on the Outlining Toolbar**	
BUTTON	**BUTTON NAME**	**DESCRIPTION**
⬅	Promote	Moves the selected paragraph to the next-higher heading level (up one level, to the left).
➡	Demote	Moves the selected paragraph to the next-lower heading level (down one level, to the right).
⬆	Move Up	Moves a selected paragraph and its collapsed (temporarily hidden) subordinate text above the preceding displayed paragraph.
⬆	Move Down	Moves a selected paragraph and its collapsed (temporarily hidden) subordinate text below the following displayed paragraph.
➖	Collapse	Hides all but the title of selected slides. Collapsed text is represented by a gray line.
➕	Expand	Displays the titles and all collapsed text of selected slides.
📑	Collapse All	Displays only the title of each slide. Text other than the title is represented by a gray line below the title.
📑	Expand All	Displays the titles and all the body text for each slide.
📑	Summary Slide	Creates a new slide from the titles of the slides you select in slide sorter or normal view. The summary slide creates a bulleted list from the titles of the selected slides. PowerPoint inserts the summary slide in front of the first selected slide.
A̲A̲	Show Formatting	Shows or hides character formatting (such as bold and italic) in normal view. In slide sorter view, switches between showing all text and graphics on each slide and displaying titles only.
◀	Toolbar Options	Allows you to select the particular buttons you want to display on the toolbar.

Creating a Presentation on the Outline Tab

The Outline tab enables you to view title and body text, add and delete slides, drag and drop slide text, drag and drop individual slides, promote and demote text, save a presentation, print an outline, print slides, copy and paste slides or text to and from other presentations, apply a design template, and import an outline. When you **drag and drop** slide text or individual slides, you change the order of the text or the slides by selecting the text or slide you want to move or copy and then dragging the text or slide it its new location.

Developing a presentation on the Outline tab is quick because you type the text for all slides on one screen. Once you type the outline, the presentation fundamentally is complete. If you choose, you then can enhance your presentation with objects in the slide pane.

Creating a Title Slide on the Outline Tab

Recall from Project 1 that the title slide introduces the presentation to the audience. In addition to introducing the presentation, Project 2 uses the title slide to capture the attention of the students in your audience by using a design template with an image of water. Perform the following steps to create a title slide on the Outline tab.

Steps **To Create a Title Slide on the Outline Tab**

1 **Click the Slide 1 slide icon on the Outline tab.**

The Slide 1 slide icon is selected. You also could click anywhere in the tabs pane to select the slide icon (Figure 2-7).

FIGURE 2-7

2 **Type** Enjoy Spring Break **and then press** SHIFT+ENTER. **Type** in the Caribbean **and then press the** ENTER **key. Point to the Demote button on the Outlining toolbar.**

The Demote ScreenTip displays (Figure 2-8). Pressing SHIFT+ENTER moves the insertion point to the next line and maintains the same first level. The insertion point is in position for typing the title for Slide 2. Pressing the ENTER key inserts a new slide.

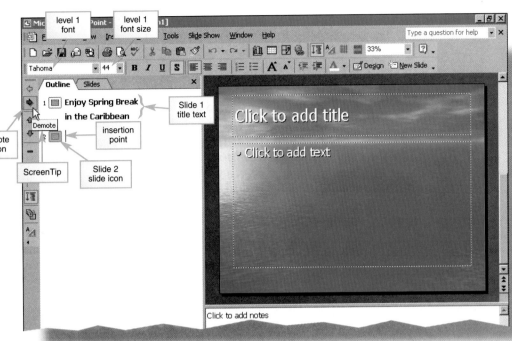

FIGURE 2-8

3 **Click the Demote button on the Outlining toolbar. Type** Warm Days, Cool Activities **and then press the** ENTER **key. Type** Sponsored by **and then press the** ENTER **key. Type** The Office of Student Activities **and then press the** ENTER **key.**

Clicking the Demote button deletes a blank slide. The two paragraphs are subtitles on the title slide (Slide 1) and demote to the second level (Figure 2-9). The second level is indented to the right below the first-level paragraph.

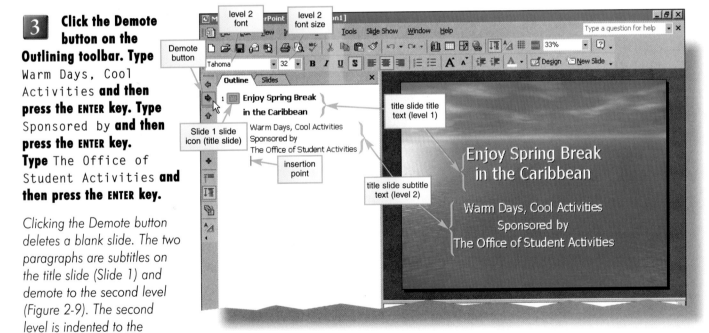

FIGURE 2-9

The title slide text for the Enjoy Spring Break presentation is complete. The next section explains how to add a slide on the Outline tab.

Other **Ways**

1. Type title text, press ENTER, click Demote button on Formatting toolbar, type subtitle text, press ENTER

2. Type title text, press ENTER, press TAB, type subtitle text, press ENTER

Adding a Slide on the Outline Tab

Recall from Project 1 that when you add a new slide in normal view, PowerPoint defaults to a Text slide layout with a bulleted list. This action occurs on the Outline tab as well. One way to add a new slide on the Outline tab is to promote a paragraph to the first level by clicking the Promote button on the Outlining toolbar until the insertion point or the paragraph displays at the first level. A slide icon displays when the insertion point or paragraph reaches this level. Perform the following step to add a slide on the Outline tab.

Steps | **To Add a Slide on the Outline Tab**

---

1 **Click the Promote button on the Outlining toolbar.**

The Slide 2 slide icon displays indicating a new slide is added to the presentation (Figure 2-10). The insertion point is in position to type the title for Slide 2 at the first level.

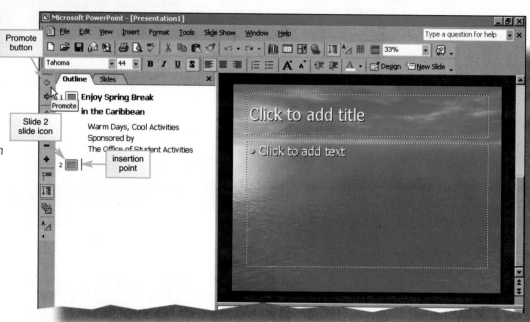

FIGURE 2-10

Other Ways

1. Click New Slide button on Standard toolbar, click OK button
2. On Insert menu click New Slide, click OK button
3. Press CTRL+M
4. Press ALT+I, press N.
5. In Voice Command mode, say "New Slide"

After you add a slide, you are ready to type the slide text. The next section explains how to create a text slide with a single-level bulleted list on the Outline tab.

Creating a Text Slide with a Single-Level Bulleted List on the Outline Tab

To create a text slide with a single-level bulleted list, you demote or promote the insertion point to the appropriate level and then type the paragraph text. Recall from Project 1 that when you demote a paragraph, PowerPoint adds a bullet to the left of each level. Depending on the design template, each level has a different bullet font. Also recall that the design template determines font attributes, including the bullet font.

Slide 2 is the first text slide in Project 2 and describes the activities students can enjoy when the cruise ship docks at various ports. Each of the four major activities displays as second-level paragraphs on the Outline tab and in the slide pane. The following steps explain how to create a text slide with a single-level bulleted list on the Outline tab.

To Create a Text Slide with a Single-Level Bulleted List

Steps **on the Outline Tab**

1 **Type** Onshore Adventures **and then press the ENTER key. Click the Demote button on the Outlining toolbar to demote to the second level.**

The title for Slide 2, Onshore Adventures, displays and the insertion point is in position to type the first bulleted paragraph (Figure 2-11). A bullet displays to the left of the insertion point.

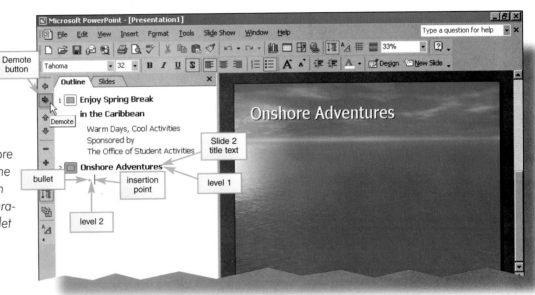

FIGURE 2-11

2 **Type** Golf, play volleyball, swim, and relax **and then press the ENTER key. Type** Experience a submarine tour **and then press the ENTER key. Type** Try parasailing **and then press the ENTER key. Type** Explore a rainforest **and then press the ENTER key.**

Slide 2 displays two levels: the title, Onshore Adventures, on the first level; and four bulleted paragraphs and the insertion point on the second level (Figure 2-12).

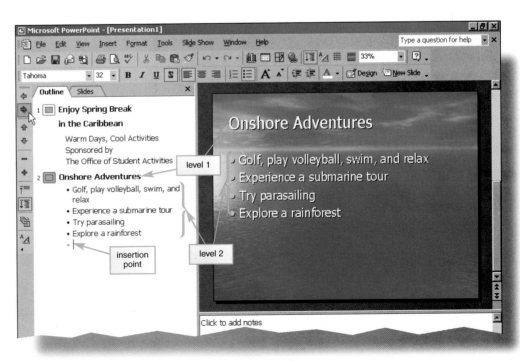

FIGURE 2-12

Slide 2 is complete. The text on this slide abides by the 7 × 7 rule. As you learned in Project 1, this rule recommends that each line should have a maximum of seven words, and each slide should have a maximum of seven lines. All slides in this slide show use the 7 × 7 rule.

Bullets

Besides using bullets, a numbered list can add emphasis to your presentation. When necessary, numbering can show ordered steps or sequences. To make a numbered list, click the Numbering button on the Formatting toolbar

Creating Text Slides with Multi-Level Bulleted Lists on the Outline Tab

The remaining three slides in the presentation contain multi-level bulleted lists. Slide 3 provides information about onboard activities, Slide 4 gives details about the cost and ports of call, and Slide 5 lists information on signing up for the cruise. It is easy and efficient to type the text for these slides on the Outline tab. Perform the following steps to create multi-level bulleted slides on the Outline tab.

Steps To Create a Text Slide with a Multi-Level Bulleted List on the Outline Tab

1 **Click the Promote button on the Outlining toolbar. Type** Onboard Activities **and then press the ENTER key. Click the Demote button on the Outlining toolbar to demote to the second level.**

The title for Slide 3, Onboard Activities, displays and the insertion point is in position to type the first bulleted paragraph (Figure 2-13). A bullet displays to the left of the insertion point in the second level.

FIGURE 2-13

2 **Type** Theaters, fitness center, and stores **and then press the ENTER key. Click the Demote button on the Outlining toolbar to demote to the third level. Type** Make new friends **and then press the ENTER key. Type** Dance to the hits **and then press the ENTER key. Click the Promote button on the Outlining toolbar to promote to the second level. Type** Indoor and outdoor pools and whirlpools **and then press the ENTER key.**

The text for Slide 3 is complete (Figure 2-14). Pressing the ENTER key begins a new paragraph at the same level as the previous paragraph.

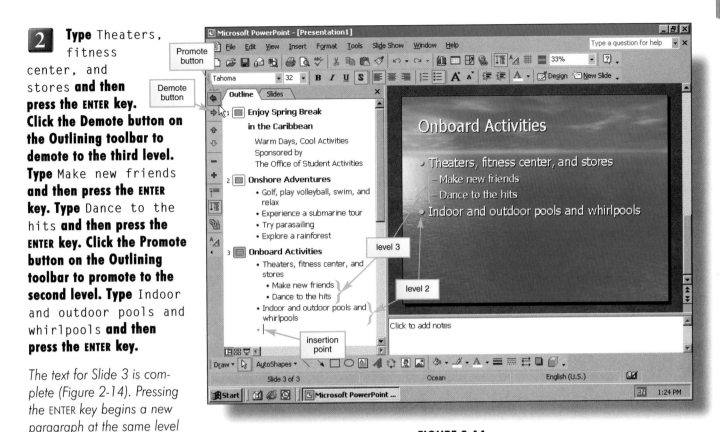

FIGURE 2-14

Entering text on the Outline tab is a quick and efficient process. You can view all the text you type in the outline in the tabs pane to check organization. The last two slides in the presentation give specific information about the cruise itinerary and registration process.

Creating a Second Text Slide with a Multi-Level Bulleted List

The next slide, Slide 4, provides details about the cost, duration, and itinerary for the cruise. Perform the following steps to create this slide.

TO CREATE A SECOND TEXT SLIDE WITH A MULTI-LEVEL BULLETED LIST

1 Click the Promote button on the Outlining toolbar so Slide 4 is added after Slide 3.

2 Type Cruise Details and then press the ENTER key.

3 Click the Demote button on the Outlining toolbar to demote to the second level.

4 Type Only $999, including all meals and then press the ENTER key.

5 Type Seven-day vacation departs from Miami and then press the ENTER key.

6 Type Unforgettable ports of call and then press the ENTER key.

7 Click the Demote button to demote to the third level.

More **About**

The Pointing Device

You can expand or collapse an outline by pointing to a heading and then holding down the SHIFT key as you rotate the wheel on the Microsoft IntelliMouse® pointing device forward or backward.

8 Type Frederiksted, St. Croix and then press the ENTER key.

9 Type San Juan, Puerto Rico and then press the ENTER key.

10 Type Charlotte Amalie, St. Thomas and then press the ENTER key.

The completed Slide 4 displays (Figure 2-15). Red wavy lines display below the words Frederiksted and Amalie to indicate those words are not found in the Microsoft main dictionary or open custom dictionaries.

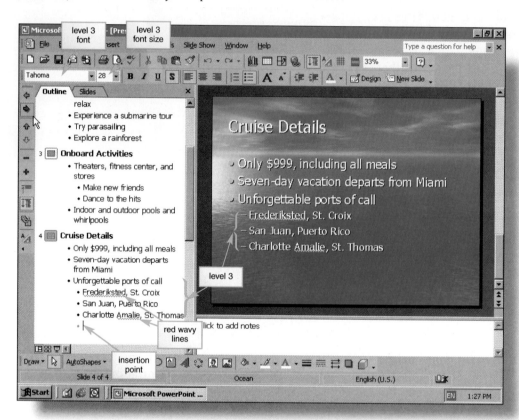

FIGURE 2-15

Creating a Closing Slide on the Outline Tab

The last slide in a presentation is the closing slide. A **closing slide** gracefully ends a presentation. Often used during a question and answer session, the closing slide usually remains on the screen to reinforce the message delivered during the presentation. Professional speakers design the closing slide with one or more of these methods.

1. List important information. Tell the audience what to do next.
2. Provide a memorable illustration or example to make a point.
3. Appeal to emotions. Remind the audience to take action or accept responsibility.
4. Summarize the main point of the presentation.
5. Cite a quotation that directly relates to the main point of the presentation. This technique is most effective if the presentation started with a quotation.

The closing slide in this project uses a multi-level bulleted list to provide contact information for the Office of Student Activities and for a reception held for students desiring additional details. Perform the following steps to create this closing slide.

Closing Slides

When faced with constructing a new slide show, you may find it helpful to start by designing your closing slide first. Knowing how you want the slide show to end helps you focus on reaching this conclusion. You can create each slide in the presentation with this goal in mind.

TO CREATE A CLOSING SLIDE ON THE OUTLINE TAB

1 Click the Promote button on the Outlining toolbar two times to add Slide 5 after Slide 4. Type Sign-Up Information and then press the ENTER key.

2 Click the Demote button on the Outlining toolbar to demote to the second level. Type Contact OSA and then press the ENTER key.

3 Click the Demote button to demote to the third level. Type Memorial Union and then press the ENTER key.

4 Click the Demote button to demote to the fourth level. Type Room 3110 and then press the ENTER key. Type 9:00 a.m. to 5:00 p.m. daily and then press the ENTER key.

5 Click the Promote button two times to promote to the second level. Type Attend Caribbean Cruise Reception then press the ENTER key.

6 Click the Demote button. Type Office of Student Activities and then press the ENTER key. Click the Demote button and then type Friday, October 10 and press the ENTER key. Type 3:00 p.m. to 5:00 p.m. but do not press the ENTER key.

More About

Backgrounds

The most popular background color is blue. Used in more than 90 percent of business presentations, this color connotes serenity, reflection, and proficiency.

The completed Slide 5 displays (Figure 2-16).

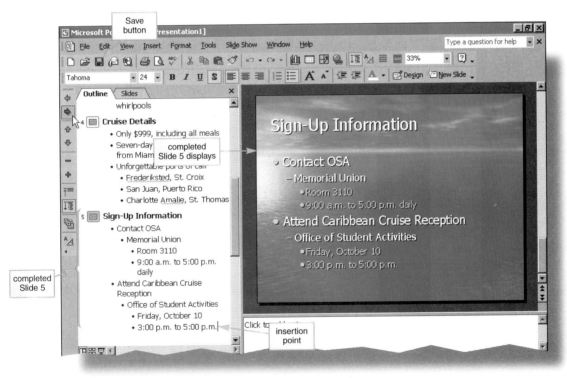

FIGURE 2-16

The outline now is complete and you should save the presentation. The next section explains how to save the presentation.

Saving a Presentation

Recall from Project 1 that it is wise to save your presentation frequently. With all the text for your presentation created, save the presentation using the steps on the next page.

TO SAVE A PRESENTATION

1 Insert a formatted floppy disk in drive A and then click the Save button on the Standard toolbar.

2 Click the Save in box arrow. Click 3½ Floppy (A:) in the Save in list.

3 Click the Save button in the Save As dialog box.

The presentation is saved on the floppy disk in drive A with the file name Enjoy Spring Break. PowerPoint uses the first text line in a presentation as the default file name. The file name displays on the title bar.

Reviewing a Presentation in Slide Sorter View

In Project 1, you displayed slides in slide show view to evaluate the presentation. Slide show view, however, restricts your evaluation to one slide at a time. The Outline tab is best for quickly reviewing all the text for a presentation. Recall from Project 1 that slide sorter view allows you to look at several slides at one time, which is why it is the best view to use to evaluate a presentation for content, organization, and overall appearance. Perform the following step to change from the Outline tab to slide sorter view.

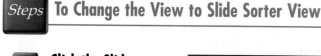

Steps **To Change the View to Slide Sorter View**

1 **Click the Slide Sorter View button** at the lower left of the PowerPoint window.

PowerPoint displays the presentation in slide sorter view (Figure 2-17). Slide 5 is selected because it was the current slide on the Outline tab. The Slide Sorter View button is selected.

FIGURE 2-17

You can review the five slides in this presentation all in one window. Notice the slides have a significant amount of space and look plain. These observations indicate a need to add visual interest to the slides by using clips. The next several sections explain how to improve the presentation by changing slide layouts and adding clip art.

You can make changes to text in normal view and on the Outline tab. It is best, however, to change the view to normal view when altering the slide layouts so you can see the result of your changes. Perform the following steps to change the view from slide sorter view to normal view.

 To Change the View to Normal View

1 **Click the Slide 2 slide thumbnail. Point to the Normal View button at the lower left of the PowerPoint window.**

Slide 2 is selected, as indicated by the thick blue border around that slide (Figure 2-18).

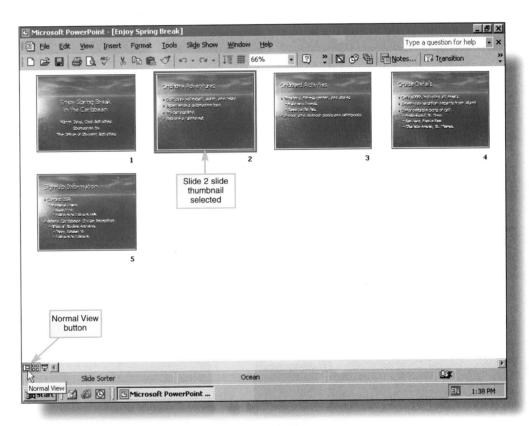

FIGURE 2-18

2 **Click the Normal View button. Point to the Slides tab in the tabs pane.**

The Normal View button is selected at the lower left of the PowerPoint window. The Slide 2 slide icon is selected in the tabs pane, and Slide 2 displays in the slide pane (Figure 2-19).

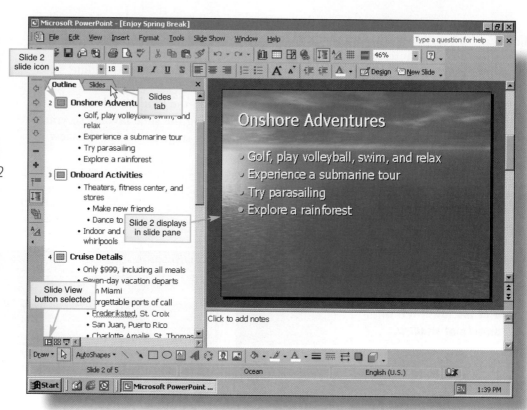

FIGURE 2-19

3 **Click the Slides tab.**

The tabs pane reduces in size. Slide thumbnails of the five slides display (Figure 2-20).

FIGURE 2-20

Switching between slide sorter view and normal view helps you review your presentation and assess whether the slides have an attractive design and adequate content.

Changing Slide Layout

When you developed this presentation, PowerPoint applied the Title Slide layout for Slide 1 and the Title and Text layout for the other four slides in the presentation. These layouts are the default styles. A **layout** specifies the arrangement of placeholders on a slide. These placeholders are arranged in various configurations and can contain text, such as the slide title or a bulleted list, or they can contain content, such as clips, pictures, charts, tables, and shapes. The placement of the text, in relationship to content, depends on the slide layout. The content placeholders may be to the right or left of the text, above the text, or below the text. You can specify a particular slide layout when you add a new slide to a presentation or after you have created the slide.

Using the **Slide Layout task pane**, you can choose a slide layout. The layouts in this task pane are arranged in four areas: Text Layouts, Content Layouts, Text and Content Layouts, and Other Layouts. The two layouts you have used in this project — Title Slide and Title and Text — are included in the Text Layouts area along with the Title Only and Title and 2-Column Text layouts. The Content Layouts area contains a blank slide and a variety of placeholder groupings for charts, tables, clip art, pictures, diagrams, and media clips. The Text and Content Layouts have placeholders for a title, a bulleted list, and content. The Other Layouts area has layouts with placeholders for a title and one object, such as clip art, charts, media clips, tables, organization charts, and charts. Some layouts have one, two, three, or four content placeholders.

When you change the layout of a slide, PowerPoint retains the text and objects and repositions them into the appropriate placeholders. Using slide layouts eliminates the need to resize objects and the font size because PowerPoint automatically sizes the objects and text to fit the placeholders. If the objects are in **landscape orientation**, meaning their width is greater than their height, PowerPoint sizes them to the width of the placeholders. If the objects are in **portrait orientation**, meaning their height is greater than their width, PowerPoint sizes them to the height of the placeholder.

Adding clips to Slides 2 and 3 requires two steps. First, change the slide layout to Title, Text, and 2 Content or to Title, Content and Text. Then, insert clip art into each of the two content placeholders. Perform the steps on the next page to change the slide layout on Slide 2 from Title and Text to Title, Text, and 2 Content.

More About

Slide Colors

One in twelve males has color perception difficulties, with the most common problem being distinguishing red and green. For more information on this color deficiency, visit the PowerPoint 2002 Project 2 More About Web page (scsite.com/pp2002/more.htm) and then click Slide Colors.

More About

Customizing Buttons

Customize your toolbars by using buttons that are larger than the ones normally displayed. To enlarge the buttons, click Tools on the menu bar and then click Customize. Click the Options tab and then click the Large icons check box. This setting will affect all of your Microsoft Office programs.

Steps To Change the Slide Layout to Title, Text, and 2 Content

1 **Click Format on the menu bar and then point to Slide Layout (Figure 2-21).**

FIGURE 2-21

2 **Click Slide Layout. Point to the Title, Text, and 2 Content layout in the Text and Content Layouts area.**

The Slide Layout task pane displays (Figure 2-22). The Title, Text, and 2 Content layout is selected, as indicated by the blue box around the template, the ScreenTip, and the arrow button on the right side.

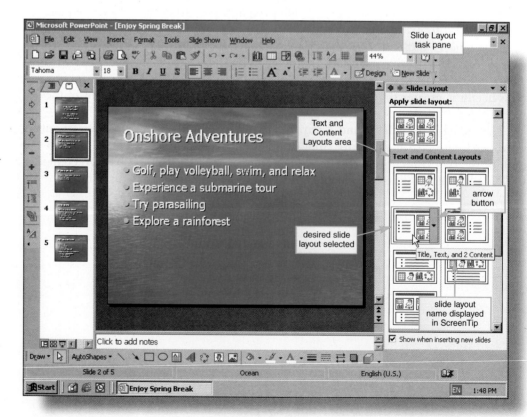

FIGURE 2-22

3 Click Title, Text, and 2 Content. Point to the Close button in the Slide Layout task pane.

The layout is applied to Slide 2 (Figure 2-23). PowerPoint moves the text placeholder containing the bulleted list to the left side of the slide and automatically resizes the text. The two content placeholders on the right side of the slide displays the message, Click icon to add content.

FIGURE 2-23

4 Click the Close button.

Slide 2 displays in normal view with the new slide layout applied (Figure 2-24).

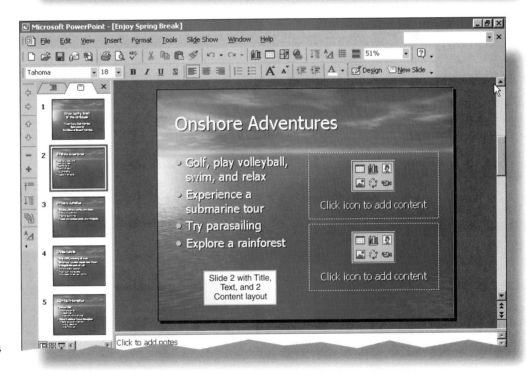

FIGURE 2-24

PowerPoint reduced the second-level text in the Slide 2 text placeholder from a font size of 32 point to 18 point so all the words fit into the placeholder.

Other Ways

1. Right-click slide anywhere except text placeholders, click Slide Layout on shortcut menu, double-click desired slide layout
2. Press ALT+O, press L, press ARROW keys to select desired slide layout, press ENTER
3. In Voice Command mode, say "Format, Slide Layout, Title Text and Two Content, Close"

Adding Clip Art to a Slide

Clip art helps the visual appeal of the Enjoy Spring Break slide show and offers a quick way to add professional looking graphic images to a presentation without creating the images yourself. This art is contained in the **Microsoft Clip Organizer**, a collection of drawings, photographs, sounds, videos, and other media files shared with Microsoft Office applications.

You can add clip art to your presentation in two ways. One way is by selecting one of the slide layouts that includes a content placeholder with instructions to open the Microsoft Clip Organizer to add content. You will add art to Slides 2 and 3 in this manner. Double-clicking a button in the content placeholder activates the instructions to open the Select Picture dialog box, which allows you to enter keywords to search for clips.

The second method is by clicking the Insert Clip Art button on the Drawing toolbar to open the Insert Clip Art task pane. The **Insert Clip Art task pane** allows you to search for clips by using descriptive keywords, file names, media file formats, and clip collections. Specific file formats could be for clip art, photographs, movies, and sounds. Clips are organized in hierarchical **clip collections**, which combine topic-related clips into categories, such as Academic, Business, and Technology. You also can create your own collections for frequently used clips. You will insert clip art into Slides 4 and 5 using this process. You then will arrange the clips on the slides without using a placeholder for content.

Table 2-2 shows four categories from the Office Collections in the Microsoft Clip Organizer and keywords of various clip art files in those categories. Clip art images have one or more keywords associated with various entities, activities, labels, and emotions. In most instances, the keywords give the name of the clip and related categories. For example, an image of a cow in the Animals category has the keywords animals, cattle, cows, dairies, farms, and Holsteins. You can enter these keywords in the Search text box to find clips when you know one of the words associated with the image. Otherwise, you may find it necessary to scroll through several categories to find an appropriate clip.

Depending on the installation of the Microsoft Clip Organizer on your computer, you may not have the clip art used in this project. Contact your instructor if you are missing clips when you perform the following steps. If you have an open connection to the Internet, clips from the Microsoft Web site will display automatically as the result of your search results.

Table 2-2	Microsoft Clip Organizer Category and Keyword Examples
CATEGORY	**CLIP ART KEYWORDS**
Academic	Books; knowledge; information; schools; school buses; apple for the teacher; professors
Business	Computers; inspirations; ideas; currencies; board meetings; conferences; teamwork; profits
Nature	Lakes; flowers; plants; seasons; wildlife; weather; trees; sunshine; rivers; leaves
Technology	Computers; diskettes; microchips; cellular telephones; e-commerce; office equipment; data exchanges

Inserting Clip Art into a Content Placeholder

With the Title, Text, and 2 Content layout applied to Slide 2, you insert clip art into the content placeholder. Perform the following steps to insert clip art of a golfer into the content placeholder on Slide 2.

Steps To Insert Clip Art into a Content Placeholder

1 **Point to the Insert Clip Art button in the top content placeholder.**

The Insert Clip Art button is selected (Figure 2-25). A ScreenTip describes its function.

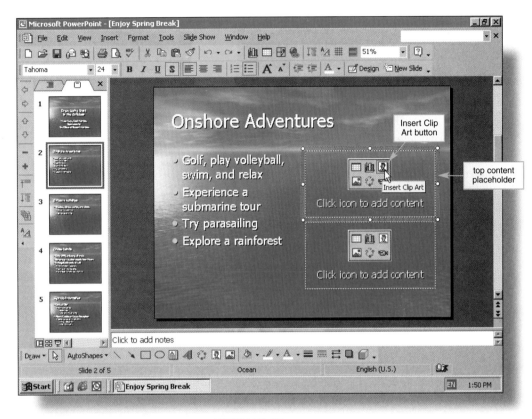

FIGURE 2-25

2 **Click the Insert Clip Art button. Type** golf **in the Search text text box and then point to the Search button.**

The Select Picture dialog box displays (Figure 2-26). The clips displayed on your computer may vary.

FIGURE 2-26

3 **Click the Search button. If necessary, click an appropriate clip and then point to the OK button.**

The Microsoft Clip Organizer searches for and displays all pictures having the keyword golf (Figure 2-27). The desired clip of a female golfer displays with a blue box around it. Your clips may be different depending on the clips installed on your computer and if you have an open connection to the Internet, in which case you may need to obtain an appropriate clip from the Internet.

FIGURE 2-27

4 **Click the OK button. If the Picture toolbar displays, click the Close button on the Picture toolbar.**

The selected clip is inserted into the top content placeholder on Slide 2 (Figure 2-28). PowerPoint sizes the clip automatically to fit the placeholder.

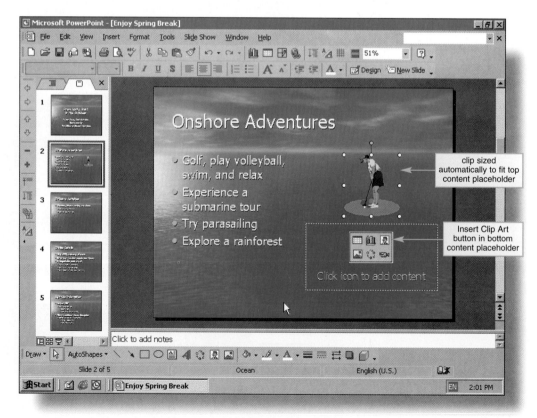

FIGURE 2-28

Inserting a Second Clip into a Slide

Another clip on Slide 2 is required to fill the bottom content placeholder. This clip should be the image of a volleyball. Perform the following steps to insert the volleyball into the bottom placeholder on Slide 2.

TO INSERT A SECOND CLIP INTO A SLIDE

1 Click the Insert Clip Art button in the bottom content placeholder.

2 Type volleyball in the Search text text box and then click the Search button.

3 If necessary, scroll down the list to display the desired clip of a volleyball and net, click the clip to select it, and then click the OK button.

The selected clip is inserted into the bottom content placeholder on Slide 2 (Figure 2-29). PowerPoint automatically sizes the clip to fit the placeholder.

More About

Design

Consider designing a presentation in black and white and then adding color to emphasize particular areas on the slide. Graphic artists suggest starting with black letters on a white background to concentrate on basic design principles, such as balance, contrast, rhythm, and harmony.

FIGURE 2-29

Slide 2 is complete. The next step is to add other clip to Slide 3. This slide uses the Title, Content and Text slide layout so the clip displays on the left side of the slide and the bulleted list displays on the right side. Perform the following steps to change the slide layout and then add clip art to Slide 3.

TO CHANGE THE SLIDE LAYOUT TO TITLE, CONTENT AND TEXT AND INSERT CLIP ART

1 Click the Next Slide button on the vertical scroll bar to display Slide 3.

2 Click Format on the menu bar and then click Slide Layout.

3 Scroll to display the Title, Content and Text slide layout located in the Text and Content Layouts area of the Slide Layout task pane.

4 Click the Title, Content and Text slide layout and then click the Close button in the Slide Layout task pane.

5   Click the Insert Clip Art button in the content placeholder. Type party in the Search text text box and then click the Search button.

6   If necessary, scroll down the list to display the desired party clip and then click the clip to select it. Click the OK button.

The selected party clip is inserted into the content placeholder on Slide 3 (Figure 2-30). The slide has the Title, Content and Text slide layout.

FIGURE 2-30

Slide 3 is complete. Your next step is to add a clip to Slide 4 without changing the slide layout.

Inserting Clip Art into a Slide without a Content Placeholder

PowerPoint does not require you to use a content placeholder to add clips to a slide. You can insert clips on any slide regardless of its slide layout. On Slides 2 and 3, you added clips that enhanced the message in the text. Recall that the slide layout on Slide 4 is Title and Text. Because this layout does not contain a content placeholder, you can use the Insert Clip Art button on the Drawing toolbar to start the Microsoft Clip Organizer. The clip for which you are searching has a globe and luggage. A few of its keywords are baggage, Earth, global, and globes. Perform the following steps to insert this clip into a slide that does not have a content placeholder.

Steps To Insert Clip Art into a Slide without a Content Placeholder

1 **Click the Next Slide button on the vertical scroll bar to display Slide 4. Click Tools on the menu bar and then click AutoCorrect Options. When the AutoCorrect dialog box displays, if necessary, click the AutoFormat As You Type tab. Click Automatic layout for inserted objects in the Apply as you work area if a check mark does not display.**

2 **Click the Insert Clip Art button on the Drawing toolbar. If the Add Clips to Organizer dialog box displays asking if you want to catalog media files, click Don't show this message again, or, if you want to catalog later, click the Later button.**

The Insert Clip Art task pane displays (Figure 2-31).

FIGURE 2-31

3 **Click the Search text text box. Type** earth **and then press the ENTER key. If necessary, scroll to display the desired clip of a globe and luggage. Point to this image.**

The clip of a globe and piece of luggage displays with other clips sharing the earth keyword (Figure 2-32). Your clips may be different. The clip's keywords, size in pixels (260 × 247), file size (10 KB), and file type (WMF) display.

FIGURE 2-32

4 | **Click the desired clip. Click the Close button on the Insert Clip Art task pane title bar.**

PowerPoint inserts the clip into Slide 4 (Figure 2-33). The slide layout changes automatically to Title, Text, and Content. The Automatic Layout Options button displays.

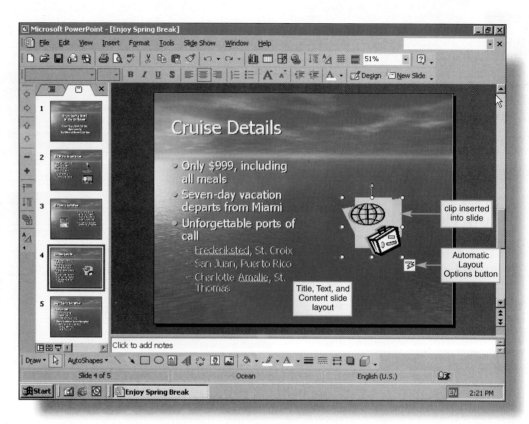

FIGURE 2-33

Table 2-3 Primary File Formats PowerPoint Recognizes	
FORMAT	*FILE EXTENSION*
Computer Graphics Metafile	.cgm
CorelDRAW	.cdr, .cdt, .cmx, and .pat
Encapsulated PostScript	.eps
Enhanced Metafile	.emf
FlashPix	.fpx
Graphics Interchange Format	.gif
Hanako	.jsh, .jah, and .jbh
Joint Photographic Experts Group (JPEG)	.jpg
Kodak PhotoCD	.pcd
Macintosh PICT	.pct
PC Paintbrush	.pcx
Portable Network Graphics	.png
Tagged Image File Format	.tif
Windows Bitmap	.bmp, .rle, .dib
Microsoft Windows Metafile	.wmf
WordPerfect Graphics	.wpg

In addition to clip art, you can insert pictures into a presentation. These may include scanned photographs, line art, and artwork from compact discs. To insert a picture into a presentation, the picture must be saved in a format that PowerPoint can recognize. Table 2-3 identifies some of the formats PowerPoint recognizes.

You can import files saved with the .emf, .gif, .jpg, .png, .bmp, .rle, .dib, and .wmf formats directly into PowerPoint presentations. All other file formats require separate filters that are shipped with the PowerPoint installation software and must be installed. You can download additional filters from the Microsoft Office Update Web site.

Smart Tags

A **smart tag** is a button that automatically appears on the screen when PowerPoint performs a certain action. The Automatic Layout Options button in Figure 2-33 is a smart tag. In addition to the Automatic Layout Options button, PowerPoint provides three other smart tags. Table 2-4 summarizes the smart tags available in PowerPoint.

Table 2-4	**Smart Tags in PowerPoint**	
BUTTON	*NAME*	*MENU FUNCTION*
[AutoCorrect Options icon]	AutoCorrect Options	Undoes an automatic correction, stops future automatic corrections of this type, or displays the AutoCorrect Options dialog box
[Paste Options icon]	Paste Options	Specifies how moved or pasted items should display, e.g., with original formatting, without formatting, or with different formatting
[AutoFit Options icon]	AutoFit Options	Undoes automatic text resizing to fit the current placeholder or changes single-column layouts to two-column layouts, inserts a new slide, or splits the text between two slides
[Automatic Layout Options icon]	Automatic Layout Options	Adjusts the slide layout to accommodate an inserted object

Clicking a smart tag button displays a menu that contains commands relative to the action performed at the location of the smart tag. For example, if you want PowerPoint to undo the layout change when you add a clip to a slide, click the Automatic Layout Options button to display the Smart Tag Actions menu, and then click Undo Automatic Layout on the Smart Tag Actions menu to display the initial layout.

Using the Automatic Layout Options Button to Undo a Layout Change

The Title and Text layout used in Slide 4 did not provide a content placeholder for the clip you inserted, so PowerPoint automatically changed the layout to Title, Text, and Content. Because the text now violates the 7 × 7 rule with this layout and because you want to place the clip in a location other than the areas specified, you should change the layout to the Title and Text layout.

The **Automatic Layout Options button** displays because PowerPoint changed the layout automatically. If you move your mouse pointer near the changed object or text, the Automatic Layout Options button displays as an arrow, indicating that a list of options is available that allow you to undo the new layout, stop the automatic layout of inserted objects, or alter the AutoCorrect Options settings. Perform the steps on the next page to undo the layout change.

Smart Tags

Microsoft PowerPoint automatically formats or corrects text as you type. For example, if you type a fraction, such as 1/4, the characters change to a fraction symbol. When you place your mouse on the symbol, the AutoCorrect Options button displays. Click the button to see the menu of choices.

More About

Layouts

Placement of text and graphics is important to a good persuasive presentation. Using the Internet for resources, tips, and articles on making clear and interesting presentations will increase your productivity. For more information on presentation design resources, visit the PowerPoint 2002 More About Web page (scsite.com/pp2002/more.htm) and then click Resources.

To Use the Automatic Layout Options Button to Undo a Layout Change

1 **Click the Automatic Layout Options button. Point to Undo Automatic Layout.**

The Automatic Layout Options list displays (Figure 2-34). Clicking Undo Automatic Layout *will reverse the layout change.*

FIGURE 2-34

2 **Click Undo Automatic Layout.**

The layout reverts to Title and Text (Figure 2-35).

FIGURE 2-35

The desired clip displays in the center of Slide 4, which has the original Title and Text slide layout. The next step is to move the clip to the bottom-right corner of the slide.

Moving Clip Art

After you insert a clip into a slide, you may want to reposition it. The globe and luggage on Slide 4 overlays the bulleted list. You want to move the clip away from the text to the bottom-right corner of the slide. First move the clip and then change its size. Perform the steps below to move the clip to the bottom-right side of the slide.

Steps **To Move Clip Art**

1 **With the clip selected, point to the clip and then click.**

2 **Press and hold down the mouse button. Drag the clip to the bottom-right corner of the slide. Release the mouse button.**

When you drag a clip, a dotted box displays. The dotted box indicates the clip's new position. When you release the left mouse button, the clip of the globe and luggage displays in the new location and the dotted line disappears (Figure 2-36). Sizing handles display at the corners and along its edges.

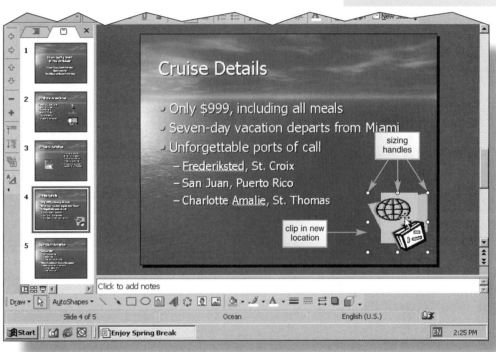

FIGURE 2-36

Changing the Size of Clip Art

Sometimes it is necessary to change the size of clip art. For example, on Slide 4 too much space displays around the clip. To make the object fit onto the slide, you increase its size. To change the size of a clip by an exact percentage, use the **Format Picture command** on the shortcut menu. The Format Picture dialog box contains six tabbed sheets with several formatting options. The **Size sheet** contains options for changing a clip's size. You either enter the exact height and width in the Size and rotate area, or enter the height and width as a percentage of the original clip in the Scale area. When the **Lock aspect ratio check box** displays a check mark, the height and width settings change to maintain the original aspect ratio. **Aspect ratio** is the relationship between an object's height and width. For example, a 3-by-5-inch object scaled to 50 percent would become a 1½-by-2½-inch object. Perform the steps on the next page to increase the size of the clip using the Format Picture dialog box.

Steps **To Change the Size of Clip Art**

1 **Right-click the clip. Point to Format Picture on the shortcut menu (Figure 2-37).**

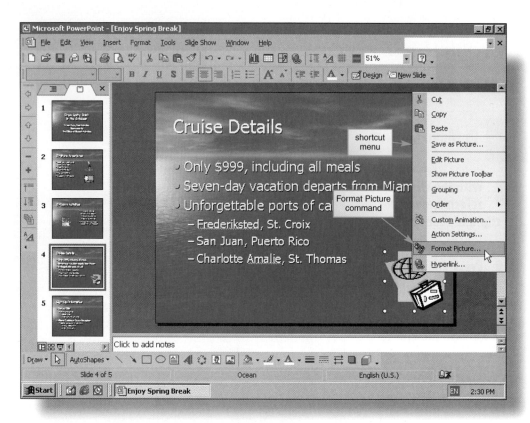

FIGURE 2-37

2 **Click Format Picture. Click the Size tab when the Format Picture dialog box displays.**

The Size sheet in the Format Picture dialog box displays (Figure 2-38). The Height and Width text boxes in the Scale area display the current percentage of the clip, 100 %. Check marks display in the Lock aspect ratio and Relative to original picture size check boxes.

FIGURE 2-38

PROJECT 2

3 Click and hold down the mouse button on the Height box up arrow in the Scale area until 125 % displays and then point to the OK button.

Both the Height and Width text boxes in the Scale area display 125 % (Figure 2-39). PowerPoint automatically changes the Height and Width text boxes in the Size and rotate area to reflect changes in the Scale area.

FIGURE 2-39

4 Click the OK button. Drag the clip to the center of the space in the bottom-right corner of the slide.

PowerPoint closes the Format Picture dialog box and displays the enlarged clip in the desired location (Figure 2-40).

Other Ways

1. Click clip, on Format menu click Picture, click Size tab, click and hold down mouse button on Height box up or down arrow in Scale area until desired size is reached, click OK button
2. Right-click slide anywhere except the text placeholders, click Slide Layout on shortcut menu, double-click desired slide layout
3. Click clip, drag a sizing handle until clip is desired shape and size
4. Press ALT+O, press I, press CTRL+TAB three times to select Size tab, press TAB to select Height text box in Scale area, press UP or DOWN ARROW keys to increase or decrease size, press ENTER

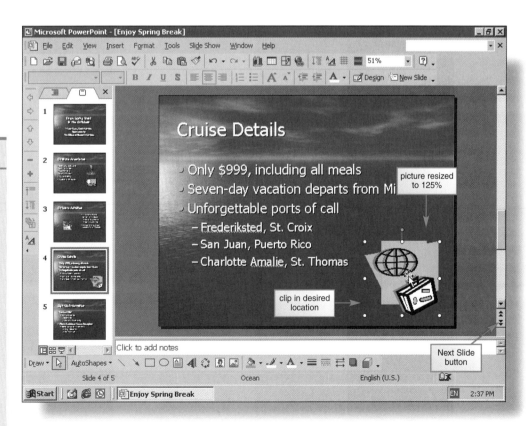

FIGURE 2-40

Inserting, Moving, and Sizing a Clip into a Slide

With Slide 4 complete, the final step is to add the alarm clock clip to the closing slide, Slide 5. Perform the following steps to add an alarm clock to Slide 5 without changing the Title and Text layout, size the clip, and then move it to the upper-right corner of the slide.

TO INSERT, MOVE, AND SIZE A CLIP INTO A SLIDE

1 Click the Next Slide button on the vertical scroll bar to display Slide 5.

2 Click the Insert Clip Art button on the Drawing toolbar. Type clock in the Search text text box and then press the ENTER key. Click the alarm clock or another appropriate clip. Click the Close button on the Insert Clip Art task pane title bar.

3 Click the Automatic Layout Options button and then click Undo Automatic Layout. Drag the clock to the upper-right corner of the slide.

4 Right-click the clock and then click Format Picture on the shortcut menu. Click the Size tab in the Format Picture dialog box, click and hold down the mouse button on the Height box up arrow in the Scale area until 150 % displays, and then click the OK button.

5 Drag the clock to the center of the space in the upper-right corner of the slide.

The alarm clock is inserted, moved, and sized into Slide 5 (Figure 2-41).

FIGURE 2-41

Choosing Clip Art

When selecting clip art, consider the direction in which the art faces. To focus the viewer's attention on the center of the slide, images should face in rather than out of the slide. For more information, visit the PowerPoint 2002 More About Web page (scsite.com/pp2002/more .htm) and then click Selecting Clip Art.

Saving the Presentation Again

To preserve the work completed, perform the following step to save the presentation again.

TO SAVE A PRESENTATION

1 Click the Save button on the Standard toolbar.

The changes made to the presentation after the previous save are saved on a floppy disk.

A default setting in PowerPoint allows for **fast saves**, which saves only the changes made since the last time you saved. To save a full copy of the complete presentation, click Tools on the menu bar, click Options on the Tools menu, and then click the Save tab. Remove the check mark in the Allow fast saves check box by clicking the check box and then click the OK button.

Adding a Header and Footer to Outline Pages

A printout of the presentation outline often is used as an audience handout. Distributing a copy of the outline provides the audience with paper on which to write notes or comments. Another benefit of distributing a copy of the outline is to help the audience see the text on the slides when lighting is poor or the room is too large. To help identify the source of the printed outline, add a descriptive header and footer. A **header** displays at the top of the sheet of paper or slide, and a **footer** displays at the bottom. Both contain specific information, such as the presenter's name or the company's telephone number. In addition, the current date and time and the slide or page number can display beside the header or footer information.

More **About**

Using Footers

Nothing can be more frustrating than having overhead transparencies of your slides get out of order when you are giving a presentation. Help keep them organized by using page numbers and the presentation name in the footer.

Using the Notes and Handouts Sheet to Add Headers and Footers

You add headers and footers to outline pages by clicking the Notes and Handouts sheet in the Header and Footer dialog box and entering the information you want to print. Perform the following steps to add the current date, header information, the page number, and footer information to the printed outline.

Steps **To Use the Notes and Handouts Sheet to Add Headers and Footers**

1 Click **View on the menu bar** and then point to **Header and Footer (Figure 2-42).**

FIGURE 2-42

2 **Click Header and Footer. Click the Notes and Handouts tab when the Header and Footer dialog box displays. Point to the Update automatically option button.**

The Notes and Handouts sheet in the Header and Footer dialog box displays (Figure 2-43). Check marks display in the Date and time, Header, Page number, and Footer check boxes. The Fixed option button is selected.

FIGURE 2-43

3 **Click the Update automatically option button and then click the Header text box. Type** Spring Break Cruise **in the Header text box. Click the Footer text box. Type** Office of Student Activities **in the Footer text box and then point to the Apply to All button (Figure 2-44).**

FIGURE 2-44

4 **Click the Apply to All button.**

PowerPoint applies the header and footer text to the outline, closes the Header and Footer dialog box, and displays Slide 5 (Figure 2-45). You cannot see header and footer text until you print the outline (shown in Figure 2-62 on page PP 2.49).

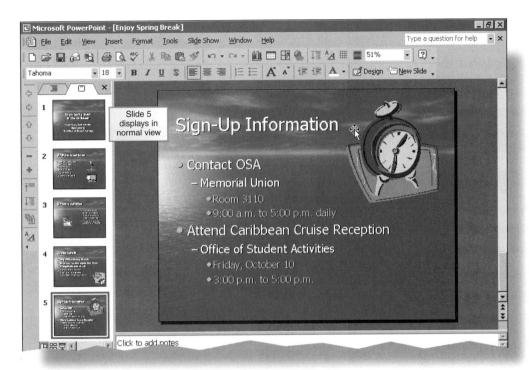

FIGURE 2-45

Applying Animation Schemes

PowerPoint provides many animation effects to add interest and make a slide show presentation look professional. **Animation** includes special visual and sound effects applied to text or content. For example, each line on the slide can swivel as it displays on the screen. Or an object can zoom in from the top of the screen to the bottom. PowerPoint provides a variety of **preset animation schemes** that determine slide transitions and effects for the title and body text. A **slide transition** is a special effect used to progress from one slide to the next in a slide show. PowerPoint also allows you to set your own **Custom animation** effects by defining your own animation types and speeds and sound effects on a slide. The following pages discuss how to add these animation effects to the presentation.

Adding an Animation Scheme to a Slide Show

PowerPoint has preset animation schemes with visual effects that vary the slide transitions and the methods in which the slide title and bullets or paragraphs display on the slides. Not all animation schemes have the slide transition element or effects for both the title and body text. These schemes are grouped in three categories: Subtle, Moderate, and Exciting. The name of the animation scheme characterizes the visual effects that display. For example, the Unfold animation scheme in the Moderate category uses the Push Right slide transition effect, the Fly In effect for the title text, and the Unfold effect for the body text. The Pinwheel scheme in the Exciting category does not use a slide transition effect, but it uses the Pinwheel effect for the title text and the Peek In effect for the body text.

More About

Animation Effects

Graphic designers suggest using a maximum of two different animation effects in one presentation. Any more than two can distract your audience from your important ideas by causing them to fixate on the visual effects and not on the slide content or the speaker. These effects should enhance your ideas in the presentation.

In this presentation, you apply the Float animation scheme to all slides. This effect is added easily by using the Slide Design task pane, which you used earlier in this project to select a design template. Perform the following steps to apply the Float animation scheme to the Enjoy Spring Break presentation.

Steps **To Add an Animation Scheme to a Slide Show**

1   **Click Slide Show on the menu bar and then point to Animation Schemes (Figure 2-46).**

FIGURE 2-46

2   **Click Animation Schemes. Scroll down the Apply to selected slides list and then point to Float in the Exciting category.**

The Slide Design task pane displays (Figure 2-47). The list of possible slide transition effects displays in the Apply to selected slides area. Exciting is one of the animation scheme categories. The Float ScreenTip shows that the Float animation scheme uses the Comb Horizontal slide transition, the Float effect for the title text, and the Descend effect for the body text.

FIGURE 2-47

3 **Click Float. Point to the Apply to All Slides button.**

PowerPoint applies the Float animation effect to Slide 5, as indicated by the animation icon on the left side of the Slide 5 slide thumbnail on the Slides tab (Figure 2-48). The Float animation effect is previewed because the AutoPreview check box is selected.

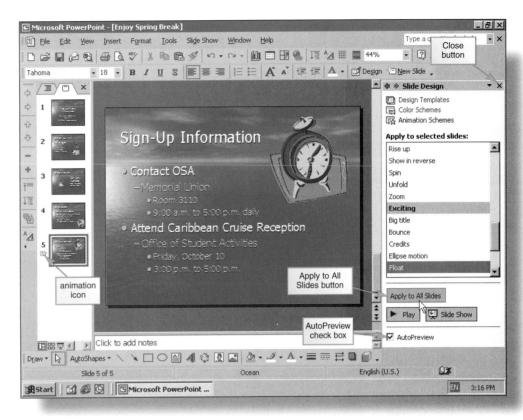

FIGURE 2-48

4 **Click Apply to All Slides. Click the Close button in the Slide Design task pane.**

The Float animation effect is applied to all slides in the presentation (Figure 2-49).

Other Ways

1. Right-click slide anywhere other than a placeholder or object, click Slide Design on shortcut menu, click Animation Schemes, select desired animation effect, click Apply to All Slides button
2. Right-click slide anywhere except text placeholders, click Slide Layout on shortcut menu, double-click desired slide layout
3. Press ALT+D, press C

FIGURE 2-49

Locating Clip Art

Thousands of public domain clips are available on the Internet. Use a search engine and the keywords, clip art and clip+art, to find these Web sites, which often contain bullets, lines, buttons, and sound files sorted into easy-to-navigate categories. You can import these files directly into your presentations.

Animating Clip Art

To add visual interest to a presentation, you can **animate** certain content. On Slide 5, for example, having the alarm clock rise from the bottom of the screen will provide a pleasing effect. Animating clip art takes several steps as described in the following sections.

Adding Animation Effects

PowerPoint allows you to animate clip art along with animating text. Because Slide 5 lists the times when students can gain additional information about the cruise, you want to emphasize these times by having the clip of the alarm clock move from the bottom of the screen to the top. One way of animating clip art is to select options in the Custom Animation dialog box. Perform the following steps to add the Flying animation effect to the clip on Slide 5.

 To Add Animation Effects

1 **Right-click the clip art image and then point to Custom Animation on the shortcut menu.**

The shortcut menu displays (Figure 2-50). The clip is selected, as indicated by the sizing handles that display at the corners and along its edges.

FIGURE 2-50

2 **Click Custom Animation. Point to the Add Effect button.**

The Custom Animation task pane displays (Figure 2-51). Two animation effects have been applied to the title and body of the slide previously.

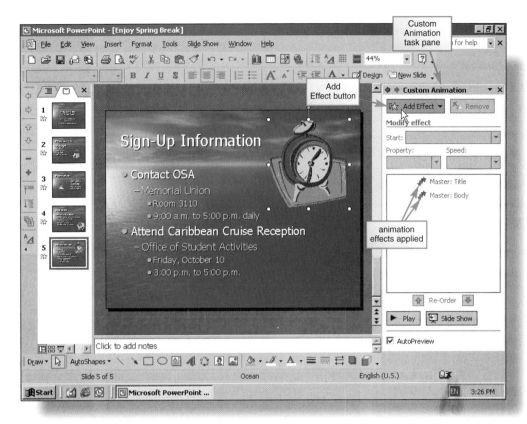

FIGURE 2-51

3 **Click the Add Effect button, point to Entrance, and then point to Fly In in the Entrance effects list.**

A list of possible effects for the Entrance option displays (Figure 2-52). Your system may display a different list of effects. You can apply a variety of effects to the clip, including how it enters and exits the slide.

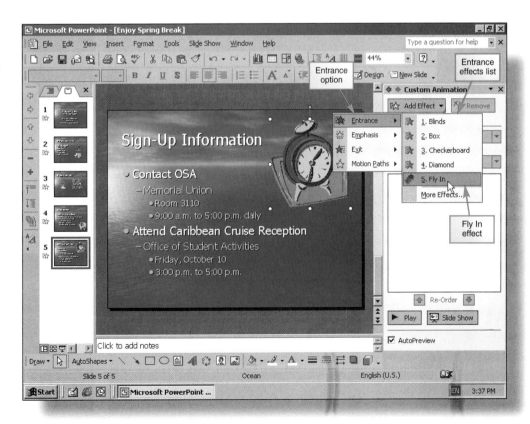

FIGURE 2-52

4 **Click Fly In. Point to the Close button on the Custom Animation task pane title bar.**

The animation effect is applied to the alarm clock, as indicated by the number 1 icon displaying to the left of the clip and the corresponding 1 displaying in the Custom Animation list (Figure 2-53). You will see this effect when you click the mouse on that slide during your slide show. J0234131 is Microsoft's internal identifier for the alarm clock clip.

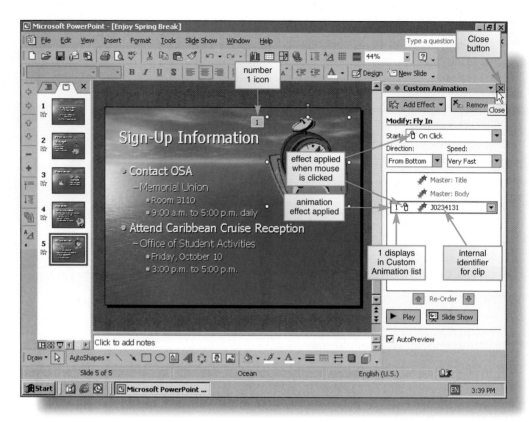

FIGURE 2-53

5 **Click the Close button (Figure 2-54).**

The alarm clock clip will appear in the presentation using the Fly In animation effect during the slide show.

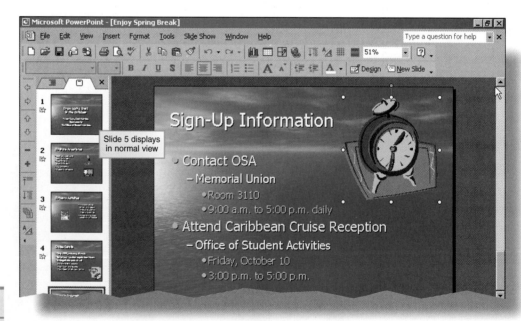

FIGURE 2-54

Other Ways

1. Click clip art, on Slide Show menu click Custom Animation, click desired animation effect, click OK button

2. Press TAB until clip art is selected, press ALT+D, press M, press DOWN ARROW key until desired animation effect selected, press ENTER

When you run the slide show, the bulleted list paragraphs will display, and then the clip art will begin moving from the bottom of the slide and stop at the position where you inserted it into Slide 5.

Animation effects are complete for this presentation. You now can review the presentation in slide show view and correct any spelling errors.

Saving the Presentation Again

The presentation is complete. Perform the following step to save the finished presentation on a floppy disk before running the slide show.

TO SAVE A PRESENTATION

1 Click the Save button on the Standard toolbar.

PowerPoint saves the presentation on your floppy disk by saving the changes made to the presentation since the last save.

Running an Animated Slide Show

Project 1 introduced you to using slide show view to look at your presentation one slide at a time. This project introduces you to running a slide show with preset and custom animation effects. When you run a slide show with slide transition effects, PowerPoint displays the slide transition effect when you click the mouse button to advance to the next slide. When a slide has text animation effects, each paragraph level displays in the sequence specified by the animation settings in the Custom Animation dialog box. Perform the following steps to run the animated Enjoy Spring Break presentation.

More About

Giving a Slide Show

If you are displaying your slide show on a projection system or external monitor, you need to match the resolutions of your computer and the projector. To do this, open the Display Properties dialog box for your computer and click the Settings tab. In the Screen area box, move the slider to adjust the resolution. If you are uncertain of the resolution, try 800 x 600 pixels. When you are using two monitors, you can display your slide show on one monitor and view your notes, outline, and slides on the second monitor.

Steps **To Run an Animated Slide Show**

1 **Click the Slide 1 slide thumbnail on the Slides tab. Click the Slide Show button at the lower left of the PowerPoint window. When Slide 1 displays in slide show view, click the slide anywhere.**

PowerPoint applies the Comb Horizontal slide transition effect and displays the title slide title text, Enjoy Spring Break in the Caribbean (Figure 2-55) using the Float animation effect. When you click the slide, the first paragraph in the subtitle text placeholder, Warm Days, Cool Activities, displays using the Descend animation effect.

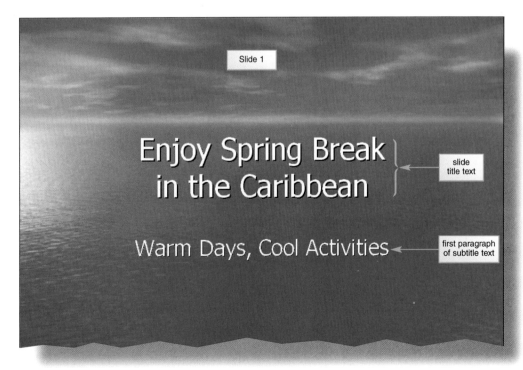

FIGURE 2-55

2 **Click the slide again.**

PowerPoint displays the second paragraph in the subtitle text placeholder, Sponsored by, using the Float animation effect (Figure 2-56). If the Popup Menu buttons display when you move the mouse pointer, do not click them.

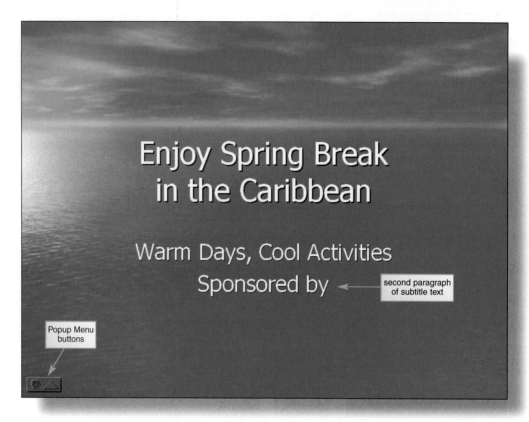

FIGURE 2-56

3 **Click the slide again.**

PowerPoint displays the third paragraph in the subtitle text placeholder, The Office of Student Activities, below the second paragraph. PowerPoint again uses the Descend animation effect (Figure 2-57).

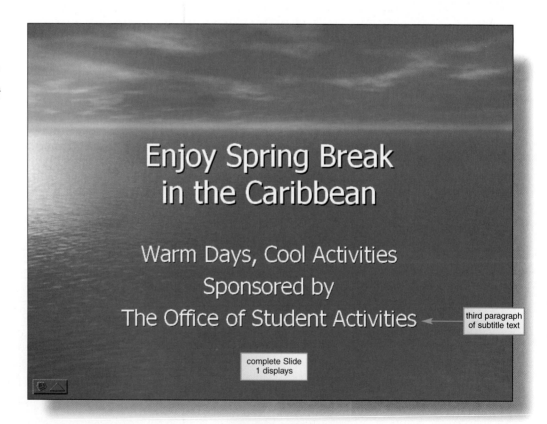

FIGURE 2-57

4 **Continue clicking to finish running the slide show and return to normal view.**

Each time a new slide displays, PowerPoint first displays the Comb Horizontal slide transition effect and only the slide title using the Float effect. Then, PowerPoint builds each slide based on the animation settings. When you click the slide after the last paragraph displays on the last slide of the presentation, PowerPoint displays a blank slide. When you click again, PowerPoint exits slide show view and returns to normal view (Figure 2-58).

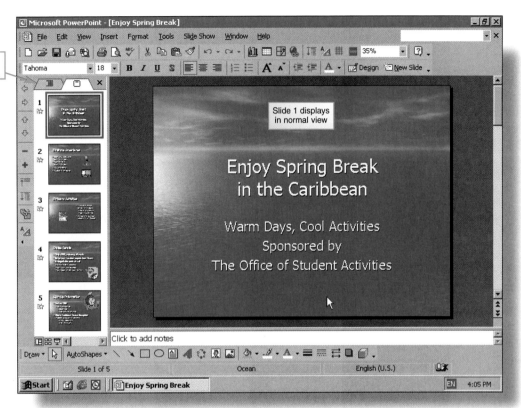

FIGURE 2-58

With the presentation complete and animation effects tested, the last step is to print the presentation outline and slides.

Printing a Presentation Created on the Outline Tab

When you click the Print button on the Standard toolbar, PowerPoint prints a hard copy of the presentation component last selected in the Print what box in the Print dialog box. To be certain to print the component you want, such as the presentation outline, use the Print command on the File menu. When the Print dialog box displays, you can select the appropriate presentation component in the Print what box. The next two sections explain how to use the Print command on the File menu to print the presentation outline and the presentation slides.

Printing an Outline

During the development of a lengthy presentation, it often is easier to review your outline in print instead of on the screen. Printing your outline also is useful for audience handouts or when your supervisor or instructor wants to review your subject matter before you develop your presentation fully.

Recall that the Print dialog box displays print options. When you want to print your outline, select Outline View in the Print what list in the Print dialog box. The outline, however, prints as last viewed on the Outline tab. This means that you must select the Zoom setting to display the outline text as you want it to print. If you are uncertain of the Zoom setting, you should return to the Outline tab and review it before printing. Perform the steps on the next page to print an outline from slide view.

Other Ways

1. On Slide Show menu click View Show, click slide until slide show ends

2. Press ALT+D, press V, press ENTER until slide show ends

3. In Voice Command mode, say "Slide Show, View Show"

More About

Sending Presentations to Word

You can create handouts and other documents by sending your PowerPoint outline to Microsoft Word and then using that text. To perform this action, click File on the menu bar, point to Send To, click Microsoft Word, and then click Outline only.

Steps **To Print an Outline**

1 **Click the Outline tab. Ready the printer according to the printer manufacturer's instructions. Click File on the menu bar and then point to Print.**

The File menu displays (Figure 2-59). The Expand All button on the Outlining toolbar is selected, so the entire outline will print. If you want to print only the slide titles, you would click the **Collapse All button** *before you click File on the menu bar.*

FIGURE 2-59

2 **Click Print on the File menu. When the Print dialog box displays, click the Print what box arrow and then point to Outline View.**

The Print dialog box displays (Figure 2-60). Outline View displays highlighted in the Print what list.

FIGURE 2-60

3   **Click Outline View in the list and then point to the OK button (Figure 2-61).**

FIGURE 2-61

4   **Click the OK button.**

To cancel the print request, click the Cancel button.

5   **When the printer stops, retrieve the printout of the outline (Figure 2-62).**

The five PowerPoint slides display in outline form. The words, Spring Break Cruise, and the current date display in the header, and the words, Office of Student Activities, and the page number display in the footer.

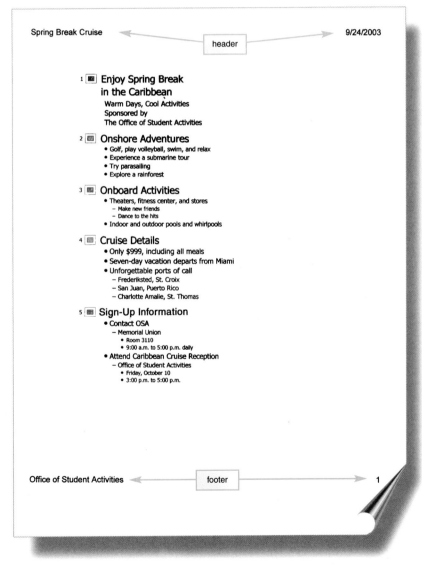

FIGURE 2-62

The **Print what list** in the Print dialog box contains options for printing slides, handouts, notes, and an outline. The Handouts area allows you to specify whether you want one, two, three, four, six, or nine slide images to display on each page. Printing handouts is useful for reviewing a presentation because you can analyze several slides displaying simultaneously on one page. Additionally, many businesses distribute handouts of the slide show before a presentation so the attendees can refer to a copy. To print handouts, click Handouts in the Print what box, click the Slides per page box arrow in the Handouts area, and then click 1, 2, 3, 4, 6, or 9. You can change the order in which the Enjoy Spring Break slides display on a page by clicking the Horizontal option button for Order in the Handouts area, which displays Slides 1 and 2, 3 and 4, and 5 and 6 adjacent to each other, or the Vertical option button for Order, which displays Slides 1 and 4, 2 and 5, and 3 and 6 adjacent to each other.

You also can click the Preview button if you want to see how your printout will look. After viewing the preview, click the Close button on the Preview window toolbar to return to normal view.

Printing Presentation Slides

At this point, you may want to check the spelling in the entire presentation and instruct PowerPoint to ignore any words spelled correctly. After correcting errors, you will want to print a final copy of your presentation. If you made any changes to your presentation since your last save, be certain to save your presentation before you print.

Perform the following steps to print the presentation.

TO PRINT PRESENTATION SLIDES

1. Ready the printer according to the printer manufacturer's instructions.

2. Click File on the menu bar and then click Print.

3. When the Print dialog box displays, click the Print what box arrow.

4. Click Slides in the list.

5. Click the OK button. When the printer stops, retrieve the slide printouts.

The printouts should resemble the slides in Figures 2-63a through 2-63e.

More About

Printing

If your printer seems to print slowly, Microsoft suggests clearing at least two megabytes of space on your hard drive and also closing any unnecessary programs that are running simultaneously.

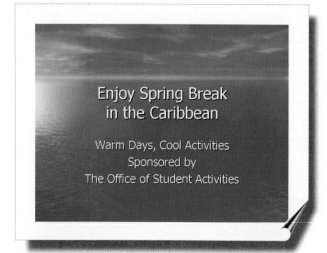

FIGURE 2-63a Slide 1

FIGURE 2-63b Slide 2

FIGURE 2-63c Slide 3

FIGURE 2-63d Slide 4

FIGURE 2-63e Slide 5

E-Mailing a Slide Show from within PowerPoint

Billions of e-mail messages are sent throughout the world each year. Computer users use this popular service on the Internet to send and receive plain text e-mail or to send and receive rich e-mail content that includes objects, links to other Web pages, and file attachments. These attachments can include Office files, such as Word documents or PowerPoint slide shows. Using Microsoft Office, you can e-mail the presentation directly from within PowerPoint.

For these steps to work properly, users need an e-mail address and a 32-bit e-mail program compatible with a Messaging Application Programming Interface, such as Outlook, Outlook Express, or Microsoft Exchange Client. Free e-mail accounts are available at hotmail.com. The steps on the next page show how to e-mail the slide show from within PowerPoint to Maria Lopez. Assume her e-mail address is maria_lopez2002@hotmail.com. If you do not have an E-mail button on the Standard toolbar, then this activity is not available to you.

More About

Sending E-Mail

Americans send more than 2.2 billion e-mail messages daily, compared with fewer than 300 million pieces of first-class mail. Professor Leonard Kleinrock sent the first e-mail message in 1969 to a colleague at Stanford University.

Steps To E-Mail a Slide Show from within PowerPoint

1 **Click the E-mail button on the Standard toolbar. When the e-mail Message window displays, type** maria_lopez2002@ hotmail.com **in the To text box. Select the text in the Subject text box and then type** Spring Break slide show **in the Subject text box. Click the message body.**

PowerPoint displays the e-mail Message window (Figure 2-64). The insertion point is in the message body so you can type a message to Maria Lopez.

FIGURE 2-64

2 **Type Attached is the PowerPoint presentation you can use to promote the Spring Break cruise. in the message body. Point to the Send button.**

The message is indented to help the recipient of the e-mail understand the purpose of your e-mail (Figure 2-65).

3 **Click the Send button on the Standard Buttons toolbar.**

The e-mail with the attached presentation is sent to maria_ lopez2002@hotmail.com.

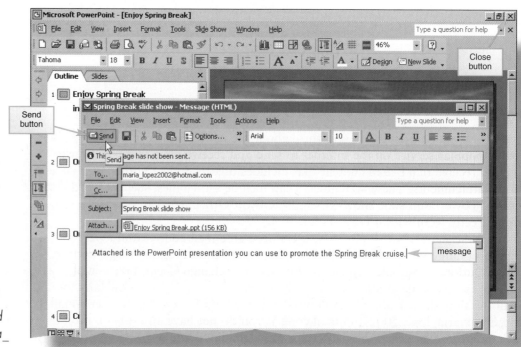

FIGURE 2-65

Because the slide show was sent as an attachment, Maria Lopez can save the attachment and then open the presentation in PowerPoint. You can choose many more options when you send e-mail from within PowerPoint. For example, the **Background command** on the Format menu changes the colors of the message background and lets you add a picture to use as the background. In addition, the **Security button** on the Standard Buttons toolbar allows you to send secure messages that only your intended recipient can read.

Saving and Quitting PowerPoint

If you made any changes to your presentation since your last save, you should save it again before quitting PowerPoint. Perform the following steps to save changes to the presentation and quit PowerPoint.

TO SAVE CHANGES AND QUIT POWERPOINT

1 Click the Close button on the Microsoft PowerPoint window title bar.

2 If prompted, click the Yes button in the Microsoft PowerPoint dialog box.

PowerPoint saves any changes made to the presentation since the last save and then quits PowerPoint.

More About

Microsoft Certification

The Microsoft Office User Specialist (MOUS) Certification program provides an opportunity for you to obtain a valuable industry credential — proof that you have the PowerPoint 2002 skills required by employers. For more information, see Appendix E or visit the Shelly Cashman Series MOUS Web page at scsite.com/offxp/cert.htm.

CASE PERSPECTIVE SUMMARY

The Enjoy Spring Break presentation should help Maria Lopez market the cruise to students at your school. These classmates viewing your presentation will learn about the onshore adventures and onboard activities and discover the details of the trip and how to find more information and register. When Maria runs your slide show, she will describe and expand upon the details you list in your slides. The audience members should have a better understanding of the cruise and the fun they can have during Spring Break this school year.

Project Summary

Project 2 introduced you to the Outline tab, clip art, and animation effects. You created a slide presentation on the Outline tab where you entered all the text in the form of an outline. You arranged the text using the Promote and Demote buttons. Once the outline was complete, you changed slide layouts and added clip art. After adding clip art to slides without using a content placeholder, you moved and sized the clips. You added preset animation effects and applied animation effects to a clip. You learned how to run an animated slide show demonstrating slide transition and animation effects. Finally, you printed the presentation outline and slides using the Print command on the File menu and e-mailed the presentation.

What You Should Know

Having completed this project, you now should be able to perform the following tasks:

▶ Add a Slide on the Outline Tab *(PP 2.12)*

▶ Add an Animation Scheme to a Slide Show *(PP 2.40)*

▶ Add Animation Effects *(PP 2.42)*

▶ Change the Size of Clip Art *(PP 2.34)*

▶ Change the Slide Layout to Title, Content and Text and Insert Clip Art *(PP 2.27)*

▶ Change the Slide Layout to Title, Text, and 2 Content *(PP 2.22)*

▶ Change the View to Normal View *(PP 2.19)*

▶ Change the View to Slide Sorter View *(PP 2.18)*

▶ Change to the Outline Tab and Display the Outlining Toolbar *(PP 2.08)*

▶ Create a Closing Slide on the Outline Tab *(PP 2.17)*

▶ Create a Second Text Slide with a Multi-Level Bulleted List *(PP 2.15)*

▶ Create a Text Slide with a Multi-Level Bulleted List on the Outline Tab *(PP 2.14)*

▶ Create a Text Slide with a Single-Level Bulleted List on the Outline Tab *(PP 2.13)*

▶ Create a Title Slide on the Outline Tab *(PP 2.10)*

▶ E-Mail a Slide Show from within PowerPoint *(PP 2.52)*

▶ Insert a Second Clip into a Slide *(PP 2.27)*

▶ Insert Clip Art into a Content Placeholder *(PP 2.25)*

▶ Insert Clip Art into a Slide without a Content Placeholder *(PP 2.29)*

▶ Insert, Move, and Size a Clip into a Slide *(PP 2.36)*

▶ Move Clip Art *(PP 2.33)*

▶ Print an Outline *(PP 2.48)*

▶ Print Presentation Slides *(PP 2.50)*

▶ Run an Animated Slide Show *(PP 2.45)*

▶ Save a Presentation *(PP 2.18, 2.37, 2.45)*

▶ Save Changes and Quit PowerPoint *(PP 2.53)*

▶ Start and Customize a New Presentation *(PP 2.06)*

▶ Use the Automatic Layout Options Button to Undo a Layout Change *(PP 2.32)*

▶ Use the Notes and Handouts Sheet to Add Headers and Footers *(PP 2.37)*

Learn It Online

Instructions: To complete the Learn It Online exercises, start your browser, click the Address bar, and then enter scsite.com/offxp/exs.htm. When the Office XP Learn It Online page displays, follow the instructions in the exercises below.

1 Project Reinforcement TF, MC, and SA

Below PowerPoint Project 2, click the Project Reinforcement link. Print the quiz by clicking Print on the File menu. Answer each question. Write your first and last name at the top of each page, and then hand in the printout to your instructor.

2 Flash Cards

Below PowerPoint Project 2, click the Flash Cards link. When Flash Cards displays, read the instructions. Type 20 (or a number specified by your instructor) in the Number of Playing Cards text box, type your name in the Name text box, and then click the Flip Card button. When the flash card displays, read the question and then click the Answer box arrow to select an answer. Flip through Flash Cards. Click Print on the File menu to print the last flash card if your score is 15 (75%) correct or greater and then hand it in to your instructor. If your score is less than 15 (75%) correct, then redo this exercise by clicking the Replay button.

3 Practice Test

Below PowerPoint Project 2, click the Practice Test link. Answer each question, enter your first and last name at the bottom of the page, and then click the Grade Test button. When the graded practice test displays on your screen, click Print on the File menu to print a hard copy. Continue to take practice tests until you score 80% or better. Hand in a printout of the final practice test to your instructor.

4 Who Wants to Be a Computer Genius?

Below PowerPoint Project 2, click the Computer Genius link. Read the instructions, enter your first and last name at the bottom of the page, and then click the Play button. Hand in your score to your instructor.

5 Wheel of Terms

Below PowerPoint Project 2, click the Wheel of Terms link. Read the instructions, and then enter your first and last name and your school name. Click the Play button. Hand in your score to your instructor.

6 Crossword Puzzle Challenge

Below PowerPoint Project 2, click the Crossword Puzzle Challenge link. Read the instructions, and then enter your first and last name. Click the Play button. Work the crossword puzzle. When you are finished, click the Submit button. When the crossword puzzle redisplays, click the Print button. Hand in the printout.

7 Tips and Tricks

Below PowerPoint Project 2, click the Tips and Tricks link. Click a topic that pertains to Project 2. Right-click the information and then click Print on the shortcut menu. Construct a brief example of what the information relates to in PowerPoint to confirm you understand how to use the tip or trick. Hand in the example and printed information.

8 Newsgroups

Below PowerPoint Project 2, click the Newsgroups link. Click a topic that pertains to Project 2. Print three comments. Hand in the comments to your instructor.

9 Expanding Your Horizons

Below PowerPoint Project 2, click the Articles for Microsoft Powerpoint link. Click a topic that pertains to Project 2. Print the information. Construct a brief example of what the information relates to in PowerPoint to confirm you understand the contents of the article. Hand in the example and printed information to your instructor.

10 Search Sleuth

Below PowerPoint Project 2, click the Search Sleuth link. To search for a term that pertains to this project, select a term below the Project 2 title and then use the Google search engine at google.com (or any major search engine) to display and print two Web pages that present information on the term. Hand in the printouts to your instructor.

Apply Your Knowledge

1 Intensifying a Presentation by Applying a Design Template, Changing Slide Layout, Inserting Clip Art, and Applying Animation Effects

Instructions: Start PowerPoint. Open the presentation Intramurals from the Data Disk. See the inside back cover of this book for instructions for downloading the Data Disk or see your instructor for information on accessing the files required for this book. Perform the following tasks to change the presentation so it looks like the slides in Figures 2-66a through 2-66d.

(a) Slide 1

(b) Slide 2

(c) Slide 3

(d) Slide 4

FIGURE 2-66

1. Apply the Teamwork design template. Add the current date and your name to the notes and handouts footer.
2. On Slide 1, increase the font size of the Indulge in Intramurals paragraph to 60 point. Insert the baseball clip shown in Figure 2-66a. Scale the clip art to 130% using the Format Picture command on the shortcut menu. Drag the baseball clip to the top center of the slide, as shown in Figure 2-66a. Apply the Diamond Entrance custom animation effect to the clip.

Apply Your Knowledge

3. Go to Slide 2. Change the slide layout to Title, 2 Content and Text. Insert the sports clips shown in Figure 2-66b. Change the size of both clips to 110%.
4. Go to Slide 3. Insert the clip shown in Figure 2-66c. Increase the clip size to 75%. Drag the clip to the bottom-right corner of the slide. Apply the Spin Emphasis custom animation effect to the clip.
5. Go to Slide 4. Change the slide layout to Title and Content over Text. Insert the telephone clip shown in Figure 2-66d and then center it between the title and the body text. Change the size of the clip to 150%. Apply the Grow/Shrink Emphasis custom animation effect to the clip. Increase the font size of the body text to 40 point.
6. Apply the Bounce animation scheme in the Exciting category list to all slides.
7. Save the presentation on a floppy disk using the file name, Intramurals Publicity.
8. Print the presentation and the outline.
9. Quit PowerPoint.

In the Lab

1 Adding Clip Art and Animation Effects to a Presentation Created on the Outline Tab

Problem: One of your assignments in your Health 101 class is to write a research paper and then share your knowledge during a five-minute presentation. You decide to research the topic of keeping your heart healthy. You generate the outline shown in Figure 2-67 to prepare the presentation. You use the outline to create the presentation shown in Figures 2-68a through 2-68d on the next page.

Instructions: Perform the following tasks.

I. Healthy Heart Hints
   A. Presented by Jennifer Korvath
   B. Health 101
II. Healthy Heart Diet
   A. General guidelines
      1) Eat foods that maintain healthy cholesterol levels
      2) Limit saturated fats
         a) In animal products
III. Exercise Benefits
   A. Aerobic activities improve cholesterol levels
      1) Brisk walking, swimming, fencing, and racquet sports
      2) May take year to see significant improvement
   B. Weight training reduces bad cholesterol levels
IV. Decrease Risk Factors
   A. Reduce stress
      1) Mental stress triggers heart disease
   B. Lose weight
      1) Obesity contributes to heart attack risk
   C. Quit smoking
      1) Responsible for 20% of heart disease deaths

FIGURE 2-67

(continued)

In the Lab

Adding Clip Art and Animation Effects to a Presentation Created on the Outline Tab *(continued)*

(a) Slide 1

(b) Slide 2

(c) Slide 3

(d) Slide 4

FIGURE 2-68

1. Use the Outline tab to create a new presentation. Apply the Digital Dots design template.

2. Using the outline shown in Figure 2-67, create the title slide shown in Figure 2-68a. Use your name instead of the name Jennifer Korvath. Decrease the font size of the class name to 28 point. Insert the heart clip art. Scale the clip to 75% and then center it at the top of the slide. Add the Box Entrance custom animation effect to the clip.

3. Using the outline in Figure 2-67, create the three text slides with bulleted lists shown in Figures 2-68b through 2-68d.

4. Change the slide layout on Slide 2 to Title, Text, and Content. Insert the heart clip art shown in Figure 2-68b. Scale the clip art to 245% and then move it to the right side of the slide. Add the Checkerboard Entrance custom animation effect to the clip.

5. Change the slide layout on Slide 3 to Title and Text over Content. Insert the clip art shown in Figure 2-68c, scale it to 215%, and then move it to the bottom left of the slide. Add the Right Motion Paths custom animation effect.

6. On Slide 4, insert the ambulance clip art shown in Figure 2-68d. Add the Box Exit custom animation effect.

In the Lab

7. Add your name to the outline header and your school's name to the outline footer.
8. Apply the Rise up animation scheme in the Moderate category to all slides in the presentation.
9. Save the presentation on a floppy disk using the file name, Healthy Heart Hints.
10. Print the presentation outline. Print the presentation.
11. Quit PowerPoint.

2 Inserting Clip Art and Animating a Slide Show

Problem: Many students at your school have asked members of the Campus Computer Club for advice on purchasing and upgrading a personal computer. To help these students best, the Club members have decided to prepare a PowerPoint presentation to show to these students. They have given you the outline shown in Figure 2-69. You create the text for the presentation on the Outline tab, and you decide to add animation effects to the slide show. The completed slides are shown in Figures 2-70a through 2-70d on the next page.

Instructions: Perform the following tasks.

1. Use the Outline tab to create a new presentation from the outline shown in Figure 2-69. Apply the Glass Layers design template.

2. On the title slide, increase the font size of Buyer's Guide to 72 point. Decrease the font size of Campus Computer Club to 28 point. Using Figure 2-70a as a reference, insert the clip art shown, scale it to 180%, and then drag it to the lower-right corner of the slide.

3. On Slide 2, insert the clip art shown in Figure 2-70b, click the AutoCorrect Options button to undo the layout change, and then drag the art to the right edge of the slide. Scale the clip to 185%.

I. Buyer's Guide
    A. Purchasing and Installing a Personal Computer
    B. Campus Computer Club
II. Determine the Type
    A. Desktop
        1) Low cost, large screen
    B. Notebook
        1) Computing capacity when you travel
    C. Handheld
        1) Handle basic organizer-type applications
III. Do Some Research
    A. Talk to friends and instructors
    B. Visit Web sites and read reviews
    C. Use a worksheet to record comparisons
IV. Make the Purchase
    A. Use a credit card
        1) Gives purchase protection, extended warranty benefits
    B. Consider an onsite service agreement
        1) Available through local dealer or third-party company
        2) Technician will arrive within 24 hours
V. Install the System
    A. Read the manuals before you start
    B. Have a well-designed work area
        1) Use ergonomic chair and keyboard

FIGURE 2-69

4. On Slide 3, change the slide layout to Title, Content and Text. Insert the clip art shown in Figure 2-70c. Scale the clip to 205% and then move it to the location show in the figure.

5. Do not make any changes to Slide 4. On Slide 5, change the slide layout to Title, Text, and Content. Insert the clip art shown in Figure 2-70e. Scale the clip to 210%.

(continued)

In the Lab

Inserting Clip Art and Animating a Slide Show (*continued*)

(a) Slide 1

(b) Slide 2

(c) Slide 3

(d) Slide 4

(e) Slide 5

FIGURE 2-70

In the Lab

6. Add the current date and your name to the outline header. Include Campus Computer Club and the page number on the outline footer.

7. Apply the Elegant animation scheme in the Moderate category to all slides.

8. Animate the clip on Slide 1 using the Blinds Entrance custom animation effect, the clip on Slide 2 using the Diagonal Down Right Motion Paths effect, the clip on Slide 3 using the Checkerboard Entrance effect, and the clip on Slide 5 using the Box Exit effect.

9. Save the presentation on a floppy disk using the file name, Buyer's Guide.

10. Print the presentation outline. Print the presentation slides. Print a handout with all five slides arranged vertically on one page.

11. Quit PowerPoint.

3 Creating a Presentation on the Outline Tab, Inserting Clip Art, and Applying Slide Transitions and Animation Effects

Problem: Chief Malcolm Snipes from the police department at your school has asked you to help him prepare a lecture on the topic of roadside emergencies. He has helped many students when they call his office for assistance. He knows that nearly 3,000 people die in car accidents every year when their cars are parked on the side of a road or on a median, and many of these fatalities started with a breakdown that could have been avoided. He asks you to prepare a PowerPoint presentation to accompany his talk. The slide show will describe how to pull off the road safely, how to obtain help, what supplies to store in your glove compartment, what supplies to keep in your trunk, and what routine maintenance you should perform. You search for appropriate clip art to add to the slides and are unable to find images that are part of the Microsoft Clip Organizer. You connect to the Internet, obtain clip from Microsoft's Web site, and create the presentation using the outline shown in Figure 2-71.

I. Handling Roadside Breakdowns
    A. Stop Problems, Remain Safe
    B. Presented by
    C. Campus Police Department
II. Pull off the Road Safely
    A. Eliminate distractions
        1) Turn off the stereo
    B. Look in mirrors
    C. Reduce speed slowly
    D. Use turn signal
        1) Not flashers
III. Obtain Help
    A. Place 'Call Police' sign in window
    B. Tie scarf or clothing to door handle or antenna
    C. Stay inside the vehicle
        1) Keep seat belt fastened
IV. Glove Compartment Supplies
    A. 'Call Police' sign
    B. Flashlight
    C. Health insurance card
    D. Pen, message pad
    E. Vehicle registration, insurance
V. Trunk Supplies
    A. Fire extinguisher
    B. Jack and lug wrench
    C. Spare tire inflated properly
    D. Jumper cables
VI. Perform Routine Maintenance
    A. Check oil level, tire pressure weekly
    B. Rotate tires every 5,000 miles
    C. Examine tires for cuts, nails, stones

FIGURE 2-71

(continued)

In the Lab

Creating a Presentation on the Outline Tab, Inserting Clip Art, and Applying Slide Transitions and Animation Effects *(continued)*

The clips you find may vary from the clips shown in Figures 2-72a through 2-72f. You then refine the presentation using clip art, animation schemes, and custom animation effects to create the slide show shown in Figures 2-72a through 2-72f.

Instructions: Perform the following tasks.

1. Create a new presentation using the Ripple design template and the outline in Figure 2-71 on the previous page.

2. On the title slide, insert the clip art shown in Figure 2-72a and add the Fly In Entrance custom animation effect. Change the speed to Slow. Size the clip if necessary.

3. On Slide 2, change the slide layout to Title, Text, and 2 Content, and insert the clips shown in Figure 2-72b. Add the Fly In Entrance custom animation effect for the top image and change the Direction to From Top-Right. Add the Fly In Entrance custom animation effect for the bottom image. Size the clips if necessary.

4. On Slide 3, change the slide layout to Title and Text over Content, and insert the clip shown in Figure 2-72c. Add the Grow/Shrink Emphasis custom animation effect. Size the clip if necessary.

5. Change the slide layout on Slide 4 (Figure 2-72d) to Title, 2 Content and Text. Insert the two clip art images shown. Add the Box Entrance custom animation effect to both clips. Size the clips if necessary.

6. On Slide 5 (Figure 2-72e), change the slide layout to Title and 2 Content over Text. Insert the clips shown and add the Fly In Entrance custom animation effect for both. Change the Direction for the fire extinguisher to From Top-Left and for the tire to From Top-Right. Size the clips if necessary.

7. On Slide 6 (Figure 2-72f), change the slide layout to Title, Text, and 2 Content. Insert the clips shown and add the Spin Emphasis custom animation effect to both. Size the clips if necessary.

8. Display your name and the current date on the outline header, and display the page number and the name of your school on the outline footer.

9. Apply the Unfold animation scheme to all slides.

10. Save the presentation on a floppy disk using the file name, Roadside Breakdowns.

11. Run the slide show.

12. Print the presentation outline. Print the presentation slides. Print a handout with all six slides arranged horizontally on one page. E-mail the presentation to Chief Snipes using the address malcolm_snipes@ hotmail.com.

13. Quit PowerPoint.

In the Lab

(a) Slide 1

(b) Slide 2

(c) Slide 3

(d) Slide 4

(e) Slide 5

(f) Slide 6

FIGURE 2-72

Cases and Places

The difficulty of these case studies varies:
▶ are the least difficult; ▶▶ are more difficult; and ▶▶▶ are the most difficult.

1 ▶ With the holidays approaching, Janis Lamata, the head librarian at Weber Hills Community Library, wants to present a series of cooking demonstrations. Janis has asked Jean-Luc Richard, the head chef at Chateau la Flambeau Restaurant, to make the presentations. His first program features grilling turkeys and is called, Grilling Is Not Just for Steaks. Jean-Luc provides the outline shown in Figure 2-73 and asks your help in creating a PowerPoint presentation. Using the concepts and techniques introduced in this project, together with Jean-Luc's outline, develop slides for a slide show. Include clip art and animation effects to add interest. Print the outline and slides as handouts so they can be distributed to presentation attendees.

I. Grilling Is Not Just for Steaks
  A. Cooking Turkeys on Your Outdoor Grill
  B. Presented by
  C. Jean-Luc Richard
  D. Head Chef, Chateau la Flambeau Restaurant
II. Before You Start
  A. Pick a turkey less than 24 pounds
    1. Make sure it is thawed completely
  B. Have plenty of fuel
    1. Propane tanks - 5 to 6 hours
    2. Charcoal - 65 to 75 briquettes
  C. Wash hands and utensils thoroughly before touching food
III. Start Cooking
  A. Set grill for indirect grilling and place bird on grill
  B. Cooking times
    1. 12-14 lbs. - 2½ to 3 hours
    2. 15-17 lbs. - 2¾ to 3½ hours
    3. 18-22 lbs. - 3½ to 4¼ hours
  C. No need to turn or baste
IV. Doneness
  A. Cook until meat thermometer reaches 180 degrees
  B. Remove from grill
  C. Let stand 20 minutes
  D. Smoked turkey may appear a little pink
    1. It is cooked thoroughly

FIGURE 2-73

Cases and Places

2 ▸ Dr. Jasmine Lopez wants to make a presentation at the Rest Haven Rehabilitation Center and Clinic where you volunteer on weekends. The presentation is a series of healthy tips for those planning to retire between the ages of 50 and 55 so they can enjoy their retirement for many years. The nursing director, Charles Becker, asks you to create a PowerPoint presentation for Dr. Lopez. The presentation will cover preventive health strategies for those planning early retirement. Dr. Lopez has provided the outline shown in Figure 2-74. Using the concepts and techniques introduced in this project, together with Dr. Lopez's outline, develop slides for a slide show. Include clip art and animation effects to add interest. Print the outline and slides as a one-page handout so they can be distributed to presentation attendees.

I. Staying Healthy as You Age
   A. Presented by
   B. Dr. Jasmine Lopez
   C. Board-certified internist and Director of Adult Health Care
II. Eating to Live Longer
   A. Balance food with physical activity
   B. Eat plenty of whole grains, vegetables, and fruits
   C. Reduce fatty meats
      1. Choose fish and chicken
      2. Concentrate on low-saturated fats
   D. Limit consumption of salt, sugar, and alcoholic beverages
III. Longevity with Vitamins
   A. B vitamins reduce homocysteine protein
      1. Decrease heart disease
   B. As we age, we have difficulty absorbing calcium and vitamins B-12 and D
   C. Vitamin C
      1. Decreases cancer risk by 20%
      2. Reduces the risk of heart attacks by 40%
IV. Do Not Call This a Diet
   A. White blood cells (natural infection fighters) are affected by what we eat
   B. Eat for life
      1. Follow the USDA Food Guide Pyramid
      2. Avoid cooking fats derived from animal products
      3. Avoid trans fats (hydrogenated fats)
         a. They increase triglycerides

FIGURE 2-74

3 ▸▸ Strength training offers many positive benefits. First, it builds power. Athletes who participate in strength training can increase their performance in other sports, such as tennis or golf. Strength training also provides energy. Research shows that strength training increases endurance for runners and swimmers. Another benefit of this training is decreased fatigue. It also improves mood, self-confidence, and self-esteem, which expand beyond sports into personal life. Strength training also helps prevent osteoporosis by strengthening bones and building bone density. It helps burn calories, even while a person is resting, by increasing the body's metabolism for as many as 12 hours after exercising. The training also balances the body by making both sides equally strong. Normally, one side is stronger than the other. A balanced body is less prone to injuries. The director of your campus fitness center wants new members to view a presentation on strength training. Using the techniques introduced in this project, create a slide show about strength training. Include appropriate clip art and animation effects.

Cases and Places

4 ▶▶ As an intern for the Great Lakes Arts Association (GLAA), you have helped the Association's director, Rajish Gupta, with many projects. He asks you to create a PowerPoint presentation for his visits at many community sites. Rajish says the Association's mission is to strengthen the bond between the diverse communities in the Great Lakes area. It also provides opportunities for artistic expression, education, cultural exchanges, and art appreciation. In addition, the Association's commission provides cultural planning, grant writing, information and referral services, and technical assistance. It sponsors exhibits of local, regional, national, and international artists at various locations. Exhibits feature fiber art, photography, paintings, folk art, glass, and sculptures. Educational opportunities include art classes and workshops by prominent artists at local schools, lectures, readings, bus tours narrated by art historians and authorities, and scholarships to send gifted students from low-income families to state colleges and private art schools. Membership levels are student, individual, family, artist, patron, sponsor, benefactor, life member, and organization. Using the techniques introduced in this project, create a presentation about the GLAA. Include appropriate clip art and animation effects.

5 ▶▶ Walking is one of the easiest methods of exercising. Many students have discovered that walking enhances both the body and spirit. Leading researchers believe this form of exercise also prolongs life. Paula Peerman, the director of recreation at your community's park district, wants to organize a walking club and has asked you to help her promote the idea. She wants you to recruit and motivate members by describing various techniques to enhance their walking routines. For example, members can try interval training by increasing their walking speed for 30 seconds and then returning to their normal speed for one minute. They also should walk with a friend to add motivation and help pass the time. If they do not feel like walking on a particular day, they can tell each other they are going to exercise for just a few minutes. Those few minutes might stretch into a half-hour or more. Walkers should swing their arms to increase their heart rates and to burn more calories. Using the techniques introduced in this project, create a presentation about the benefits of walking. Include appropriate clip art and animation effects.

6 ▶▶▶ Bookstores are becoming an integral part of the community. Many have guest speakers, cultural events, and various clubs. Your local bookstore, Bobbie's Books, is sponsoring a book club, where members will meet on four consecutive Monday nights to discuss a famous author. Pick a prominent author, such as Stephen King, Danielle Steel, John Grisham, Michael Crichton, or Margaret Eleanor Atwood. Visit your local bookstore and library, and search the Internet for information about the author. Then, create a presentation to promote Bobbie's Books. Include a short biography of this author, describe his or her best-selling books, discuss critical comments by reviewers, and present relevant Web sites. Include appropriate clip art and animation effects.

7 ▶▶▶ Many homeowners are finding the cost of remodeling prohibitive, so they are taking on do-it-yourself projects. Visit two local lumberyards or building supply stores and collect information about adding a wooden deck to a home. Learn about the different types of wood and stains, the various types of designs, and how to maintain the deck. Then, create a PowerPoint presentation that includes a summary of this information along with a list of the tools and materials needed and the estimated time to complete the project. Add appropriate clip art and animation effects.

Microsoft PowerPoint 2002

Creating a Presentation on the Web Using PowerPoint

CASE PERSPECTIVE

With the Internet transforming the job market, corporations are rethinking the way they advertise their available jobs and market their businesses on Web sites. They list their open positions and describe the positive aspects of their companies on their corporate Web sites. Job seekers, likewise, are changing their traditional methods of searching for jobs and marketing themselves. They now prepare electronic or online resumes and send them via e-mail to businesses. They also search for jobs on employment Web sites, called job boards, such as Monster.com.

The Placement Center director at Highland College, Tina Natella, wants to teach students how to use the Internet to find careers. She decides the most effective way to disseminate this information is to have you prepare a PowerPoint slide show and then make the presentation available on the World Wide Web to all students. The slide show, called Job Search, will contain this information along with clip art and an animation scheme for visual interest. Tina then wants you to publish the presentation on the Web in a file named Jobs on the Internet.

Introduction

The graphic design power of PowerPoint allows you to create vibrant presentations that convey information in a clear, interesting manner. Some of these presentations are created for small, specific audiences, such as a subcommittee planning a department retreat. In this case, the presentation may be shown in an office conference room. Other presentations are designed for large, general audiences, such as workers at a corporation's various offices across the country learning about a new insurance benefits package. These employees can view the presentation on their company's **intranet**, which is an internal network that uses Internet technologies. On a grand scale, you can inform the entire world about the contents of your presentation by posting your slide show to the World Wide Web. To publish to the World Wide Web, you need an **FTP (File Transfer Protocol)** program to copy your presentation and related files to a Web server.

PowerPoint allows you to create a Web page in two ways. First, you can start a new presentation, as you did in Projects 1 and 2 when you produced the Make Friends and Enjoy Spring Break presentations. PowerPoint provides a Web Presentation template in the **AutoContent Wizard** option when you start PowerPoint. The wizard provides design and content ideas to help you develop an effective slide show for an intranet or for the Internet by opening a sample presentation that you can alter by adding your own text and graphics.

Second, by using the **Save as Web Page command**, you can convert an existing presentation to a format compatible with popular Web browsers such as Microsoft Internet Explorer. This command allows you to create a Web page from a single slide or from a multiple-slide presentation.

This Web Feature illustrates opening the Job Search presentation on the Data Disk (Figure 1a) and then saving the presentation as a Web page using the Save as Web Page command. See the inside back cover of this book for instructions for downloading the Data Disk or see your instructor for information on accessing the files required in this book. Then, you will publish your presentation, and PowerPoint will start your default browser and open your HTML file so you can view the presentation (Figures 1b through 1e). Finally, you will edit the presentation, save it again, and view it again in your default browser.

FIGURE 1

You can preview your presentation as a Web page. This action opens the presentation in your default Web browser without saving HTML files. You can use this feature to review and modify your work in progress until you develop a satisfactory presentation.

Because you are converting the Job Search presentation on the Data Disk to a Web page, the first step in this project is to open the Job Search file. Then, you will save the file as a Web page and view the presentation in your default browser. For instructional purposes in this Web Feature, you create and save your Web page on a floppy disk. At times, this saving process may be slow, so you must be patient.

More *About*

Job Searches on the Internet

Corporations are predicted to spend $4 billion by 2005 on online recruiting and job-placement advertisements, up from $411 million in 1999. Newspaper classified advertising revenues are expected to decrease dramatically. Some human resources personnel claim they can fill vacant positions twice as quickly by posting their ads online rather than placing ads in the newspaper.

Saving a PowerPoint Presentation as a Web Page

Once a PowerPoint slide show is complete, you want to save it as a Web page so you can publish and then view it in a Web browser. Microsoft Internet Explorer and Netscape Navigator are the two more common browsers installed on computers today. PowerPoint allows you to **publish** the presentation by saving the pages to a Web folder or to an FTP location. When you publish your presentation, it is available for other computer users to view on the Internet or by other means.

You can save and then view the presentation in two ways. First, you can save the entire presentation as a Web page, quit PowerPoint, open your browser, and open the Web page in your browser. Second, you can combine these steps by saving the presentation as a Web page, publishing the presentation, and then viewing the presentation as a Web page. In this case, PowerPoint will start the browser and display your presentation automatically. Perform the following steps to save and publish the Job Search presentation as a Web page.

 To Save a PowerPoint Presentation as a Web Page

1 **Start PowerPoint and then open the Job Search file on the Data Disk. Click the notes pane and then type** The Internet empowers job seekers to find the jobs or careers that best fit their interests and goals. **as the note. Click File on the menu bar and then point to Save as Web Page.**

PowerPoint opens and displays the presentation in normal view (Figure 2). The File menu displays. The notes frame contains the speaker notes you typed.

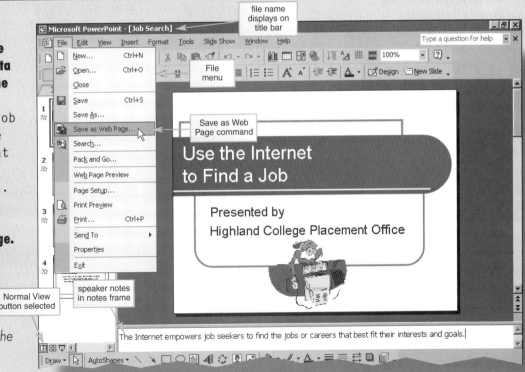

FIGURE 2

2 **Click Save as Web Page. When the Save As dialog box displays, type** Jobs on the Internet **in the File name text box. Point to the Publish button.**

PowerPoint displays the Save As dialog box (Figure 3). Web Page displays in the Save as type box.

FIGURE 3

3 **Click the Publish button. If the Office Assistant displays, click No, don't provide help now. When the Publish as Web Page dialog box displays, triple-click the File name text box in the Publish a copy as area and then type** A:\Jobs on the Internet **in the text box. If necessary, click Open published Web page in browser to select it. Point to the Publish button.**

The Publish as Web Page dialog box displays (Figure 4). PowerPoint defaults to publishing the complete presentation, although you can choose to publish one or a range of slides. The **Open published Web page in browser check box** *is selected, which means the Jobs on the Internet presentation will open in your default browser when you click the Publish button.*

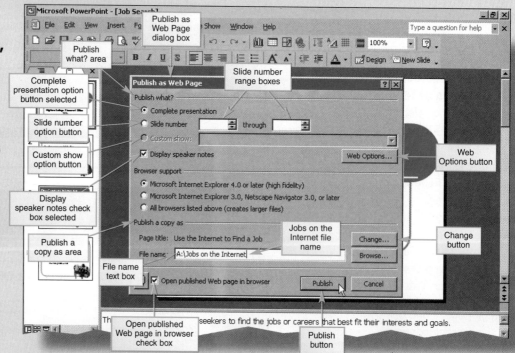

FIGURE 4

4 **Click the Publish button.**

PowerPoint saves the presentation as Jobs on the Internet.htm on the Data Disk in drive A. After a few seconds, PowerPoint opens your default Web browser in a separate window (Figure 5).

FIGURE 5

Publishing provides customizing options that are not available when you merely save the entire presentation and then start your browser. The **Publish as Web Page dialog box** provides several options to customize your Web page. For example, you can change the page title that displays on the browser's title bar and in the history list. People visiting your Web site can store a link to your Web page, which will display in their favorites list. To change the page title, you click the Change button in the Publish a copy as area (shown in Figure 4) and then type a new title.

The **Publish what? area** of the Publish as Web Page dialog box allows you to publish parts of your presentation. PowerPoint defaults to publishing the complete presentation, but you can select specific slides by clicking the **Slide number option button** and then entering the range of desired slide numbers in the range boxes. In addition, you can publish a custom show you have created previously. A **custom show** is a subset of your presentation that contains slides tailored for a specific audience. For example, you may want to show Slides 1, 2, and 4 to one group and Slides 1, 3, and 4 to another group.

You can choose to publish only the publication slides, and not the accompanying speaker notes. By default, the **Display speaker notes check box** is selected in the Publish what? area. You typed speaker notes for Slide 1 of this presentation, so they will display in the browser window. If you do not want to make your notes available to users, click the Display speaker notes check box to remove the check mark.

The **Web Options button** in the Publish what? area allows you to select options to determine how your presentation will look when viewed in a Web browser. You can choose options such as allowing slide animation to show, selecting the screen size, and having the notes and outline panes display when viewing the presentation in a Web browser.

With the Job Search file opened and the presentation saved as a Web page, the next step is to view the slide show using your default browser.

Other Ways

1. Press ALT+F, press G, type new file name, press SHIFT+TAB two times, press P, change file name in Publish copy as area; press ENTER

2. In Voice Command mode, say "File, Save as Web Page, [type file name], Publish, [type file name], Publish"

More About

Publishing Web Presentations

One advantage of publishing a PowerPoint presentation is the flexibility of using Web discussions to gather comments about the document. Saving the presentation as an .htm or .mht Web-based format provides the most flexibility for reviewers. The .mht format combines multiple pictures and slides into a single file called a Web archive. For more information, visit the PowerPoint 2002 More About Web page (scsite.com/pp2002/more.htm) and then click Publishing.

Viewing a Presentation

Presentations to large groups or distributed over many sites can create problems. Publishing the presentation as a Web page allows individuals to see the slides, but recording a broadcast for later viewing on the Internet is another alternative. For more information, visit the PowerPoint 2002 More About Web page (scsite.com/pp2002/more.htm) and then click Broadcasting.

Viewing a Presentation as a Web Page

PowerPoint makes it easy to create a presentation and then view how it will display on an intranet or the World Wide Web. By viewing your slide show, you can decide which features look good and which need modification. The left side of the window contains the navigation frame, which is the outline of the presentation. The outline displays a table of contents consisting of each slide's title text. You can click the **Expand/Collapse Outline button** below the navigation frame to view the complete slide text. The right side of the window displays the complete slide in the slide frame. The speaker notes display in the notes frame below the slide frame. Perform the following steps to view the Jobs on the Internet presentation as a Web page.

Steps To View a Presentation as a Web Page

1 **Double-click the Microsoft Internet Explorer title bar to maximize the browser window. Point to the Full Screen Slide Show button.**

Slide 1 of the Jobs on the Internet presentation displays in the slide frame in the browser window (Figure 6). The navigation frame contains the table of contents, which consists of the title text of each slide. The notes frame displays the speaker notes.

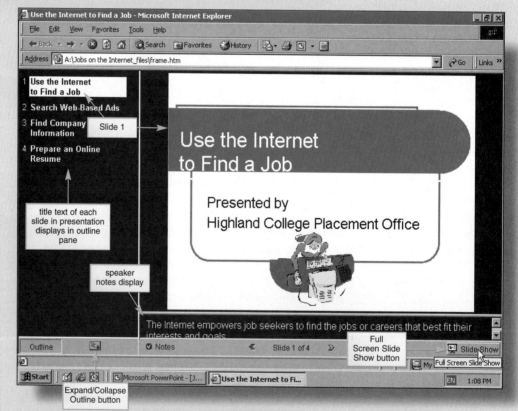

FIGURE 6

2 Click the Full Screen Slide Show button.

Slide 1 fills the entire screen (Figure 7). The Slide 1 title text and computer clip art display.

Use the Internet
to Find a Job

FIGURE 7

3 Click to display the first line of the subtitle text.

The first line of the Slide 1 subtitle text displays.

4 If necessary, continue clicking each slide in the presentation. When the black slide displays, click it. Click the Yes button in the Microsoft PowerPoint dialog box. Point to the Expand/Collapse Outline button below the outline.

Each of the four slides in the Jobs on the Internet presentation displays. The message on the black slide, End of slide show, click to exit., indicates the conclusion of the slide show.

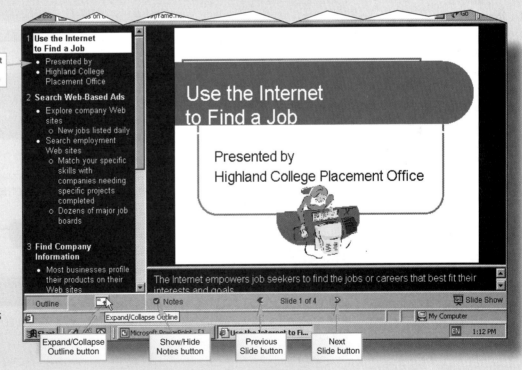

FIGURE 8

5 Click the Expand/Collapse Outline button.

The navigation frame displays the text of each slide in an outline (Figure 8). To display only the title of each slide, you would click the Expand/Collapse Outline button again.

You can alter the browser window by choosing to display or hide the navigation and notes frames. To hide the navigation frame, click the **Show/Hide Outline button** below the outline. Later, if you want to redisplay the navigation frame, click the Show/Hide Outline button again. Similarly, the **Show/Hide Notes button** below the slide frame allows you to display or conceal the speaker notes on a particular slide.

To advance through the Web page, click the **Next Slide button** below the slide frame. Likewise, to display a slide appearing earlier in the slide show, click the **Previous Slide button**.

Editing a Web Page through a Browser

You may want to modify your Web page by making small changes to the text or art on some slides. In this presentation, you want to change the title text in Slide 1 to reflect the fact that the presentation covers more than finding a job on the Internet; it describes various resources available for planning a career. The following steps change the second line of the title slide to modify Slide 1.

Steps To Edit a Web Page through a Browser

1 **Point to the Edit button** on the **Standard Buttons toolbar.**

Slide 1 displays in the browser (Figure 9). The ScreenTip, Edit with Microsoft PowerPoint, indicates you can modify the presentation using PowerPoint directly in the browser window. Your computer may indicate other editing options, such as using Windows Notepad.

FIGURE 9

2 **Click the Edit button. Select the words, Find a Job, in the second line of the title text placeholder.**

When you click the Edit button, PowerPoint opens a new presentation with the same file name as the Web presentation file name, as indicated by the title bar and the recessed PowerPoint Jobs on the Internet button on the Windows taskbar (Figure 10). A selection rectangle displays around the title text place-holder. The three words are highlighted.

FIGURE 10

3 **Type** Locate Job Resources **and then point to the Save button on the Standard toolbar.**

The second line is modified (Figure 11).

FIGURE 11

4 **Click the Save button. Point to the Use the Internet to Find a Job – Microsoft Internet Explorer button on the taskbar.**

PowerPoint saves the changes to the Jobs on the Internet.htm file on the Data Disk in drive A. The buttons on the taskbar indicate that two PowerPoint presentations and the browser are open (Figure 12).

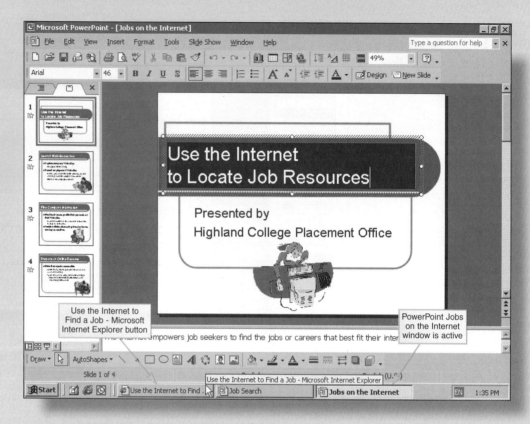

FIGURE 12

5 **Click the Use the Internet to Find a Job – Microsoft Internet Explorer button and then point to the Refresh button on the Standard Buttons toolbar.**

The browser window displays the title text and clip art on Slide 1 (Figure 13). The Refresh button displays the most current version of the Web page.

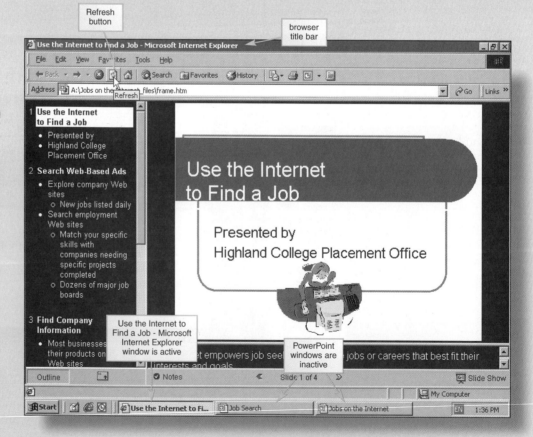

FIGURE 13

6 **Click the Refresh button. Point to the Close button on the browser title bar.**

The complete Slide 1 displays with the editing change (Figure 14).

7 **Click the Close button.**

PowerPoint closes the Jobs on the Internet Web presentation, and the PowerPoint window redisplays in normal view with the Jobs on the Internet presentation active.

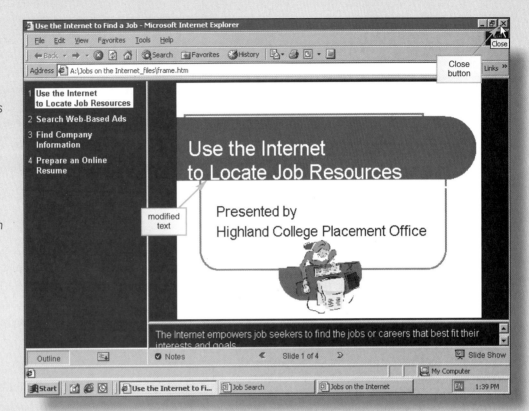

FIGURE 14

The Web page now is complete. The next step is to make your Web presentation available to others on your network, an intranet, or the World Wide Web. Ask your instructor how you can post your presentation.

CASE PERSPECTIVE SUMMARY

Students attending Tina Natella's presentation in the Placement Center should learn information on using the Internet to improve their career searches. The Job Search slide show will help to reinforce the key points presented, including facts about searching Web-based advertisements, finding company information, and preparing an online resume. The students will be able to apply this information when they look for a first job or a new career. Tina can publish your presentation to the World Wide Web so that students who cannot attend the lecture also can gain the useful information presented.

Web Feature Summary

This Web feature introduced you to creating a Web page by saving an existing PowerPoint presentation as an HTML file. You then viewed the presentation as a Web page in your default browser. Next, you modified Slide 1. Finally, you reviewed the Slide 1 change using your default browser. With the Job Search presentation converted to a Web page, you can post the file to an intranet or to the World Wide Web.

What You Should Know

Having completed this Web Feature, you now should be able to perform the following tasks:

▶ Edit a Web Page through a Browser *(PPW 1.08)*
▶ Save a PowerPoint Presentation as a Web Page *(PPW 1.03)*
▶ View a Presentation as a Web Page *(PPW 1.06)*

In the Lab

1 Creating a Web Page from the Make Friends Presentation

Problem: Jennifer Williams, the dean of counseling at Westview College, wants to expand the visibility of the Make Friends presentation you created for the counseling department in Project 1. She believes the World Wide Web would be an excellent vehicle to help students throughout the campus and at other colleges, and she has asked you to help transfer the presentation to the Internet.

Instructions: Start PowerPoint and then perform the following steps with a computer.

1. Open the Make Friends presentation shown in Figures 1-2a through 1-2d on page PP 1.09 that you created in Project 1. (If you did not complete Project 1, see your instructor for a copy of the presentation.)
2. Use the Save as Web Page command on the File menu to convert and publish the presentation. Save the Web page using the file name, Curing Loneliness.
3. View the presentation in a browser.
4. Modify Slide 2 by adding the words, on Campus, to the title.
5. Change the first third-level paragraph to the words, Current events, sports scores, on Slide 4.
6. View the modified Web page in a browser.
7. Ask your instructor for instructions on how to post your Web page so others may have access to it.

2 Creating a Web Page from the Enjoy Spring Break Presentation

Problem: The Enjoy Spring Break presentation you developed in Project 2 for the Office of Student Activities is generating much interest. Students are visiting the office, which has moved to Room 3221, and requesting longer hours for the Caribbean Cruise Reception. Maria Lopez, the student activities director, has asked you to post the presentation to the school's intranet.

Instructions: Start PowerPoint and then perform the following steps with a computer.

1. Open the Enjoy Spring Break presentation shown in Figures 2-1a through 2-1e on page PP 2.05 that you created in Project 2. (If you did not complete Project 2, see your instructor for a copy of the presentation.)
2. Use the Save as Web Page command on the File menu to convert and publish the presentation. Save the Web page using the file name, Caribbean Cruise.
3. View the presentation in a browser.
4. Modify Slide 2 by changing the word, parasailing, to the words, scuba diving, in the third bulleted paragraph.
5. Modify Slide 5 by changing the room number to 3221 and by changing the ending time of the reception to 8:00 p.m.
6. View the modified Web page in a browser.
7. Ask your instructor for instructions on how to post your Web page so others may have access to it.

In the Lab

3 Creating a Personal Presentation

Problem: You have decided to apply for an internship at a not-for-profit organization in Chicago. You are preparing to send your resume and cover letter to the executive director, and you want to develop a unique way to publicize your computer expertise. You decide to create a personalized PowerPoint presentation emphasizing your leadership abilities and scholarly achievements. You refer to this presentation in your cover letter and inform the executive director that she can view this presentation because you have saved the presentation as a Web page and posted the pages on your school's server.

Instructions: Start PowerPoint and then perform the following steps with a computer.

1. Prepare a presentation highlighting your leadership abilities. Create a title slide and at least three additional slides. Use appropriate clip art and an animation scheme.
2. Use the Save as Web Page command to convert and publish the presentation. Save the Web page using the file name, Additional Skills.
3. View the presentation in a browser.
4. Ask your instructor for instructions on how to post your Web page so others may have access to it.

APPENDIX A
Microsoft PowerPoint Help System

Using the PowerPoint Help System

This appendix shows you how to use the PowerPoint Help system. At anytime while you are using PowerPoint, you can interact with its Help system and display information on any PowerPoint topic. It is a complete reference manual at your fingertips.

As shown in Figure A-1, you can access PowerPoint's Help system in four primary ways:

1. Ask a Question box on the menu bar
2. Function key F1 on the keyboard
3. Microsoft PowerPoint Help command on the Help menu
4. Microsoft PowerPoint Help button on the Standard toolbar

If you use the Ask a Question box on the menu bar, PowerPoint responds by opening the Microsoft PowerPoint Help window, which gives you direct access to its Help system. If you use one of the other three ways to access PowerPoint's Help system, PowerPoint responds in one of two ways:

1. If the Office Assistant is turned on, then the Office Assistant displays with a balloon (lower-right side in Figure A-1).
2. If the Office Assistant is turned off, then the Microsoft PowerPoint Help window opens (lower-left side in Figure A-1).

FIGURE A-1

The best way to familiarize yourself with the PowerPoint Help system is to use it. The next several pages show examples of how to use the Help system. Following the examples is a set of exercises titled Use Help that will sharpen your PowerPoint Help system skills.

Ask a Question Box

The **Ask a Question box** on the right side of the menu bar lets you type questions in your own words, or you can type terms, such as animation scheme, Outline tab, or bulleted list. PowerPoint responds by displaying a list of topics related to the term(s) you entered. The following steps show how to use the Ask a Question box to obtain information on bullet styles.

Steps **To Obtain Help Using the Ask a Question Box**

1 **Click the Ask a Question box on the right side of the menu bar, type** bullet styles, **and then press the ENTER key. Point to the Change the bullet style in a list link in the Ask a Question list.**

The Ask a Question list displays (Figure A-2). Your list may display with different entries. Clicking the See more link displays additional links.

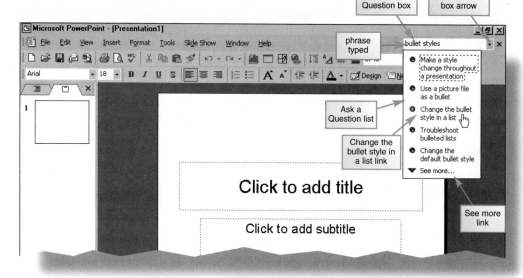

FIGURE A-2

2 **Click Change the bullet style in a list. When the Microsoft PowerPoint Help window displays, double-click its title bar to maximize it. Click the Contents tab on the Contents sheet. Point to the Change the bullet style for a single list link.**

PowerPoint opens a Microsoft PowerPoint Help window that provides information about changing bullet styles (Figure A-3).

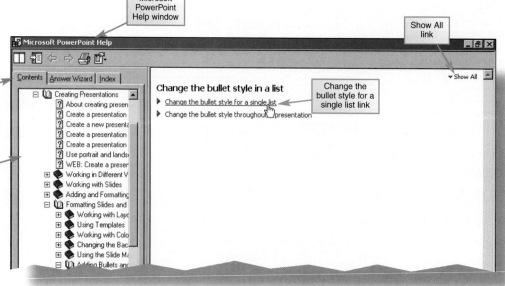

FIGURE A-3

3 **Click Change the bullet style for a single list. Read the information on this topic. Point to the Close button on the Microsoft PowerPoint Help window title bar.**

The Microsoft PowerPoint Help window provides information about changing the bullet style in a list (Figure A-4). You can click the links in item three to obtain additional information on changing the bullet character, size, or color.

4 **Click the Close button.**

The Microsoft PowerPoint Help window closes and the presentation is active.

FIGURE A-4

If the Contents sheet is active on the left side of the Microsoft PowerPoint Help window, then PowerPoint opens the book pertaining to the topic for which you are requesting help. In this case, PowerPoint opens the Formatting Slides and Presentations book and the Adding Bullets and Numbering book, which includes a list of topics related to bullets. If the information on the right side is not satisfactory, you can click one of the topics in the Contents sheet to display alternative information related to bullet styles.

As you enter questions and terms in the Ask a Question box, PowerPoint adds them to its list. Thus, if you click the Ask a Question box arrow, a list of previously asked questions and terms will display.

Use the six buttons in the upper-left corner of the Microsoft PowerPoint Help window (Figure A-4) to navigate through the Help system, change the display, and print the contents of the window. Table A-1 lists the function of each of these buttons.

Table A-1	Microsoft PowerPoint Help Toolbar Buttons	
BUTTON	**NAME**	**FUNCTION**
	Auto Tile	Tiles the Microsoft PowerPoint Help window and Microsoft PowerPoint window when the Microsoft PowerPoint Help window is maximized
or	Show or Hide	Displays or hides the Contents, Answer Wizard, and Index tabs
	Back	Displays the previous Help topic
	Forward	Displays the next Help topic
	Print	Prints the current Help topic
	Options	Displays a list of commands

The Office Assistant

The **Office Assistant** is an icon (lower-right side of Figure A-1 on page PP A.01) that displays in the PowerPoint window when it is turned on and not hidden. It has dual functions. First, it will respond in the same way the Ask a Question box does with a list of topics relating to the entry you make in the text box at the bottom of the balloon. The entry can be in the form of a word, phrase, or question written as if you were talking to a human. For example, if you want to learn more about saving a presentation, you can type any of the following terms or phrases in the balloon text box: save, save a presentation, how do I save a presentation, or anything similar. The Office Assistant responds by displaying a list of topics from which you can choose. Once you choose a topic, it displays the corresponding information.

Second, the Office Assistant monitors your work and accumulates tips during a session on how you might increase your productivity and efficiency. You can view the tips at anytime. The accumulated tips display when you activate the Office Assistant balloon. Also, if at anytime you see a lightbulb above the Office Assistant, click it to display the most recent tip.

You may or may not want the Office Assistant to display on the screen at all times. You can hide it and then show it at a later time. You may prefer not to use the Office Assistant at all. Thus, not only do you need to know how to show and hide the Office Assistant, you also need to know how to turn the Office Assistant on and off.

Showing and Hiding the Office Assistant

When PowerPoint initially is installed, the Office Assistant may be off. You turn on the Office Assistant by clicking the **Show the Office Assistant command** on the Help menu. If the Office Assistant is on the screen and you want to hide it, you click the **Hide the Office Assistant command** on the Help menu. You also can right-click the Office Assistant to display its shortcut menu and then click the **Hide command** to hide it. You can move it to any location on the screen. You can click it to display the Office Assistant balloon, which allows you to request Help.

Turning the Office Assistant On and Off

The fact that the Office Assistant is hidden does not mean it is turned off. To turn the Office Assistant off, it must be displaying in the PowerPoint window. You right-click it to display its shortcut menu (right side of Figure A-5). Next, click Options on the shortcut menu. When you click the **Options command**, the **Office Assistant dialog box** displays (left side of Figure A-5).

FIGURE A-5

In the **Options sheet** in the Office Assistant dialog box, the **Use the Office Assistant check box** at the top of the sheet determines whether the Office Assistant is on or off. To turn the Office Assistant off, remove the check mark from the Use the Office Assistant check box and then click the OK button. As shown in Figure A-1 on page PP A.01, if the Office Assistant is off when you invoke Help, then PowerPoint opens the Microsoft PowerPoint Help window instead of displaying the Office Assistant. To turn the Office Assistant on later, click the **Show the Office Assistant command** on the Help menu.

Through the Options command on the Office Assistant shortcut menu, you can change the look and feel of the Office Assistant. For example, you can hide the Office Assistant, turn the Office Assistant off, change the way it works, choose a different Office Assistant icon, or view an animation of the current one. These options also are available by clicking the **Options button** that displays in the Office Assistant balloon (Figure A-6).

The **Gallery sheet** (Figure A-5) in the Office Assistant dialog box allows you to change the appearance of the Office Assistant. The default is the paper clip (Clippit). You can change it to a bouncing red happy face (The Dot), a robot (F1), the Microsoft Office logo (Office Logo), a magician (Merlin), the earth (Mother Nature), a cat (Links), or a dog (Rocky).

Using the Office Assistant

As indicated earlier, the Office Assistant allows you to enter a word, phrase, or question and then responds by displaying a list of topics from which you can choose to display Help. The following steps show how to use the Office Assistant to obtain Help on changing a slide design.

Steps To Use the Office Assistant

1 **If the Office Assistant is not turned on, click Help on the menu bar and then click Show the Office Assistant. Click the Office Assistant. When the Office Assistant balloon displays, type** how do i change a slide layout **in the text box immediately above the Options button. Point to the Search button.**

The Office Assistant balloon displays as shown in Figure A-6.

FIGURE A-6

2 **Click the Search button. When the Office Assistant balloon redisplays, point to the topic, Apply a slide layout (Figure A-7).**

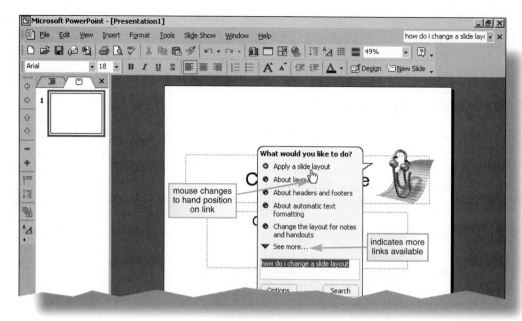

FIGURE A-7

3 **Click the topic, Apply a slide layout. If necessary, move or hide the Office Assistant so you can view all of the text in the Microsoft PowerPoint Help window.**

The Microsoft PowerPoint Help window displays the information on applying a slide layout (Figure A-8).

4 **Click the Close button on the Microsoft PowerPoint Help window title bar to close Help.**

FIGURE A-8

The Microsoft PowerPoint Help Window

If the Office Assistant is turned off and you click the Microsoft PowerPoint Help button on the Standard toolbar, the Microsoft PowerPoint Help window opens (Figure A-9). The left side of this window contains three tabs: Contents, Answer Wizard, and Index. Each tab displays a sheet with powerful look-up capabilities.

Use the Contents sheet as you would a table of contents at the front of a book to look up Help. The Answer Wizard sheet answers your queries the same as the Office Assistant. You use the Index sheet in the same fashion as an index in a book to look up Help. Click the tabs to move from sheet to sheet.

Besides clicking the Microsoft PowerPoint Help button on the Standard toolbar, you also can click the Microsoft PowerPoint Help command on the Help menu, or press the F1 key to display the Microsoft PowerPoint Help window to gain access to the three sheets. To close the Microsoft PowerPoint Help window, click the Close button in the upper-right corner on the title bar.

Using the Contents Sheet

The **Contents sheet** is useful for displaying Help when you know the general category of the topic in question, but not the specifics. The following steps show how to use the Contents sheet to obtain information on printing in black and white.

TO OBTAIN HELP USING THE CONTENTS SHEET

1 With the Office Assistant turned off, click the Microsoft PowerPoint Help button on the Standard toolbar (shown in Figure A-6 on page PP A.05).

2 When the Microsoft PowerPoint Help window displays, double-click the title bar to maximize the window. If necessary, click the Show button to display the tabs.

3 Click the Contents tab. Click the Printing Presentations book on the left side of the window.

4 Click the subtopic, About printing in black and white, below the Printing Presentations book (Figure A-9).

5 Close the Microsoft PowerPoint Help window.

PowerPoint displays Help on the subtopic, About printing in black and white (Figure A-9).

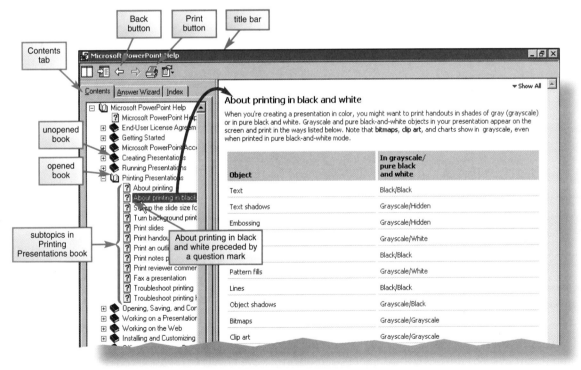

FIGURE A-9

Once the information on the subtopic displays, you can scroll through and read it or you can click the Print button to obtain a printed copy. If you decide to click another subtopic on the left or a link on the right, you can get back to the Help page shown in Figure A-9 by clicking the Back button.

Each topic in the Contents list is preceded by a book icon or question mark icon. A **book icon** indicates subtopics are available. A **question mark icon** means information on the topic will display if you double-click the title. The book icon opens when you double-click the book (or its title) or click the plus sign (+) to the left of the book icon.

Using the Answer Wizard Sheet

The **Answer Wizard sheet** works like the Office Assistant in that you enter a word, phrase, or question and it responds by listing topics from which you can choose to display Help. The following steps show how to use the Answer Wizard sheet to obtain Help on using clip art contained in the Microsoft Clip Organizer.

TO OBTAIN HELP USING THE ANSWER WIZARD SHEET

1 With the Office Assistant turned off, click the Microsoft PowerPoint Help button on the Standard toolbar (shown in Figure A-6 on page PP A.05).

2 When the Microsoft PowerPoint Help window displays, double-click the title bar to maximize the window. If necessary, click the Show button to display the tabs.

3 Click the Answer Wizard tab. Type use clip art in the What would you like to do? text box on the left side of the window and then click the Search button.

4 When a list of topics displays in the Select topic to display list, click Rotate an object (Figure A-10). Click the Rotate to any angle link on the right side of the Microsoft PowerPoint Help window.

5 Close the Microsoft PowerPoint Help window.

PowerPoint displays Help on the topic, Rotate an object (Figure A-10).

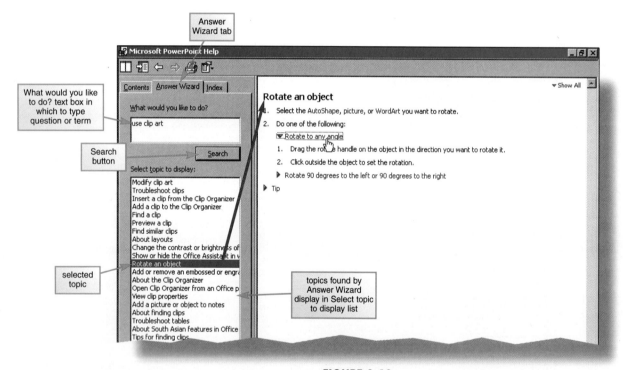

FIGURE A-10

If the topic, Rotate an object, does not include the information you are seeking, you can click another topic in the list. Continue to click topics until you find the desired information.

Using the Index Sheet

The third sheet in the Microsoft PowerPoint Help window is the Index sheet. Use the **Index sheet** to display Help when you know the keyword or the first few letters of the keyword you want to look up. The following steps show how to use the Index sheet to obtain Help on adding sounds to animated text or objects.

What's This? Command and Question Mark Button • PP A.09

APPENDIX A

TO OBTAIN HELP USING THE INDEX SHEET

1 With the Office Assistant turned off, click the Microsoft PowerPoint Help button on the Standard toolbar (shown in Figure A-6 on page PP A.05).

2 When the Microsoft PowerPoint Help window displays, double-click the title bar to maximize the window. If necessary, click the Show button to display the tabs.

3 Click the Index tab. Type animation in the Type keywords text box on the left side of the window. Click the Search button.

4 When a list of topics displays in the Choose a topic list, click Add a sound to an animation (Figure A-11).

5 Close the PowerPoint Help window.

PowerPoint displays Help on selecting sounds in the Custom Animation task pane (Figure A-11).

FIGURE A-11

An alternative to typing a keyword in the Type keywords text box is to scroll through the Or choose keywords list (the middle list on the left side of the window). When you locate the keyword you are searching for, double-click it to display Help on the topic. Also in the Or choose keywords list, the PowerPoint Help system displays other topics that relate to the new keyword. As you begin typing a new keyword in the Type keywords text box, PowerPoint jumps to that point in the middle list box. To begin a new search, click the Clear button.

What's This? Command and Question Mark Button

Use the What's This? command on the Help menu or the Question Mark button in a dialog box when you are not sure what an object on the screen is or what it does.

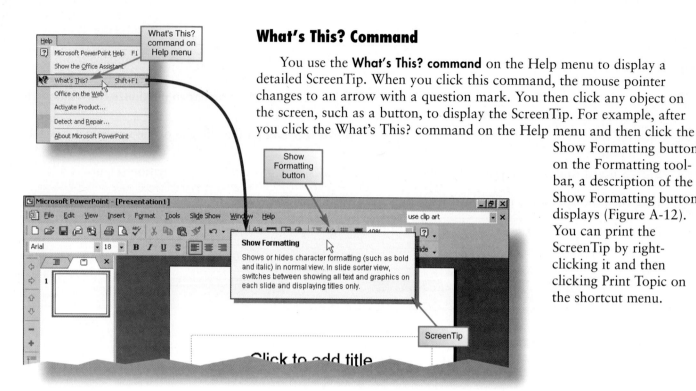

What's This? Command

You use the **What's This? command** on the Help menu to display a detailed ScreenTip. When you click this command, the mouse pointer changes to an arrow with a question mark. You then click any object on the screen, such as a button, to display the ScreenTip. For example, after you click the What's This? command on the Help menu and then click the Show Formatting button on the Formatting toolbar, a description of the Show Formatting button displays (Figure A-12). You can print the ScreenTip by right-clicking it and then clicking Print Topic on the shortcut menu.

FIGURE A-12

Question Mark Button

Similarly to the What's This? command, the **Question Mark button** displays a ScreenTip. You use the Question Mark button with dialog boxes. It is located in the upper-right corner on the title bar of dialog boxes, next to the Close button. For example, in Figure A-13, the Save As dialog box displays on the screen. If you click the Question Mark button in the upper-right corner of the dialog box and then click the Save as type box, an explanation displays. You can print the ScreenTip by right-clicking it and then clicking Print Topic on the shortcut menu.

If a dialog box does not include a Question Mark button, press SHIFT+F1. This combination of keys displays an explanation or changes the mouse pointer to an arrow with a question mark. You then can click any object in the dialog box to display the ScreenTip.

FIGURE A-13

Office on the Web Command

The **Office on the Web command** on the Help menu displays a Microsoft Web page containing up-to-date information on a variety of Office-related topics. To use this command, you must be connected to the Internet. When you invoke the Office on the Web command, the Assistance Center Home page displays. Read through the links that in general pertain to topics that relate to all Office XP topics. Scroll down and click the PowerPoint link in the Help By Product area to display the Assistance Center PowerPoint Help Articles Web page (Figure A-14). This Web page contains numerous helpful links related to PowerPoint.

FIGURE A-14

Other Help Commands

Three additional commands available on the Help menu are Activate Product, Detect and Repair, and About Microsoft PowerPoint.

Activate Product Command

The **Activate Product command** on the Help menu lets you activate PowerPoint if it has not already been activated.

Detect and Repair Command

Use the **Detect and Repair command** on the Help menu if PowerPoint is not running properly or if it is generating errors. When you invoke this command, the Detect and Repair dialog box displays. Click the Start button in the dialog box to initiate the detect and repair process.

About Microsoft PowerPoint Command

The **About Microsoft PowerPoint command** on the Help menu displays the About Microsoft PowerPoint dialog box. The dialog box lists the owner of the software and the product identification. You need to know the product identification if you call Microsoft for assistance. The three buttons below the OK button are the System Info button, the Tech Support button, and the Disabled Items button. The **System Info button** displays system information, including hardware resources, components, software environment, and applications. The **Tech Support button** displays a Microsoft PowerPoint window with product support services information. The **Disabled Items button** allows you to enable items that prevented PowerPoint from functioning correctly.

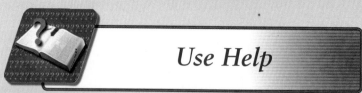

Use Help

1 Using the Ask a Question Box

Instructions: Perform the following tasks using the PowerPoint Help system.

1. Click the Ask a Question box on the menu bar, type how do i change the color scheme, and then press the ENTER key.
2. Click Modify a color scheme in the Ask a Question list. Double-click the Microsoft PowerPoint Help window title bar. Read and print the information. One at a time, click each of the three links in item two on the right side of the window to learn about modifying color schemes for slides, notes, and handouts. Print the information. Hand in the printouts to your instructor. Click the Close button in the Microsoft PowerPoint Help window.
3. Click the Ask a Question box and then press the ENTER key. Click Change text color in the Ask a Question list. If this list does not display, click the See more link and then click Change text color. When the Microsoft PowerPoint Help window displays, maximize the window.
4. Click the Show button on the Help toolbar to display the tabs. Click the Contents tab. Read and print the information. Click each of the two items on the right side of the Microsoft PowerPoint Help window; Change text color in a placeholder, AutoShape, or text box; and Change text color in WordArt. Print the information for each. Close the Microsoft PowerPoint Help window.

2 Expanding on the PowerPoint Help System Basics

Instructions: Use the PowerPoint Help system to understand the topics better and answer the questions listed below. Answer the questions on your own paper, or hand in the printed Help information to your instructor.

1. Right-click the Office Assistant. If it is not turned on, click Show the Office Assistant on the Help menu. When the shortcut menu displays, click Options. Click Use the Office Assistant to remove the check mark, and then click the OK button.
2. Click the Microsoft PowerPoint Help button on the Standard toolbar. Maximize the Microsoft PowerPoint Help window. If the tabs are hidden on the left side, click the Show button on the Help toolbar. Click the Index tab. Type slide show in the Type keywords text box. Click the Search button. Click Add transitions between slides. Print the information. Click the Hide button and then the Show button on the Help toolbar. Click the two links below Do one of the following. Read and print the information for each link. Close the Microsoft PowerPoint Help window. Hand in the printouts to your instructor.
3. Press the F1 key. Maximize the Microsoft PowerPoint Help window. Click the Answer Wizard tab. Type speech recognition in the What would you like to do? text box, and then click the Search button. Click Things you can do and say with speech recognition. Read the information that displays. Print the information. Click the two links in item one, Using Voice Command mode and Using Dictation mode. Read and print the information for both.
4. Click the Contents tab. Click the plus sign (+) to the left of the Creating Presentations book, and then click the plus sign to the left of the Adding Clip Art book. One at a time, click the first three topics below the Adding Clip Art book. Read and print each one. Close the Microsoft PowerPoint Help window. Hand in the printouts to your instructor.

APPENDIX B
Speech and Handwriting Recognition

Introduction

This appendix discusses how you can create and modify worksheets using Office XP's new input technologies. Office XP provides a variety of **text services**, which enable you to speak commands and enter text in an application. The most common text service is the keyboard. Two new text services included with Office XP are speech recognition and handwriting recognition.

When Windows was installed on your computer, you specified a default language. For example, most users in the United States select English (United States) as the default language. Through text services, you can add more than 90 additional languages and varying dialects such as Basque, English (Zimbabwe), French (France), French (Canada), German (Germany), German (Austria), and Swahili. With multiple languages available, you can switch from one language to another while working in PowerPoint. If you change the language or dialect, then text services may change the functions of the keys on the keyboard, adjust speech recognition, and alter handwriting recognition.

The Language Bar

You know that text services are installed properly when the Language Indicator button displays by the clock in the tray status area on the Windows taskbar (Figure B-1a) or the Language bar displays on the screen (Figure B-1b or B-1c). If the Language Indicator button displays in the tray status area, click it, and then click the **Show the Language bar command** (Figure B-1a). The Language bar displays on the screen in the same location it displayed last time.

You can drag the Language bar to any location in the window by pointing to its move handle, which is the vertical line on its left side (Figure B-1b). When the mouse pointer changes to a four-headed arrow, drag the Language bar to the desired location.

(a) **Language Indicator Button in Tray Status Area on Windows Taskbar and Its Menu**

(b) **Language Bar with Text Labels Disabled**

(c) **Language Bar with Text Labels Enabled**

FIGURE B-1

If you are sure that one of the services was installed and neither the Language Indicator button nor the Language bar displays, then do the following:

1. Click Start on the Windows taskbar, point to Settings, click Control Panel, and then double-click the Text Services icon in the Control Panel window.
2. When the Text Services dialog box displays, click the Language Bar button, click the Show the Language bar on the desktop check box to select it, and then click the OK button in the Language Bar Settings dialog box.
3. Click the OK button in the Text Services dialog box.
4. Close the Control Panel window.

You can perform tasks related to text services by using the **Language bar**. The Language bar may display with just the icon on each button (Figure B-1b) or it may display with text labels to the right of the icon on each button (Figure B-1c). Changing the appearance of the Language bar will be discussed shortly.

Buttons on the Language Bar

The Language bar shown in Figure B-2a contains eight buttons. The number of buttons on your Language bar may be different. These buttons are used to select the language, customize the Language bar, control the microphone, control handwriting, and obtain help.

When you click the **Language Indicator button** on the far left side of the Language bar, the Language Indicator menu displays a list of the active languages (Figure B-2b) from which you can choose. The **Microphone button**, the second button from the left, enables and disables the microphone. When the microphone is enabled, text services adds two buttons and a balloon to the Language toolbar (Figure B-2c). These additional buttons and the balloon will be discussed shortly.

The third button from the left on the Language bar is the Speech Tools button. The **Speech Tools button** displays a menu of commands (Figure B-2d) that allow you to hide or show the balloon on the Language bar; train the Speech Recognition service so that it can better interpret your voice; add and delete words from its dictionary, such as names and other words not understood easily; and change the user profile so more than one person can use the microphone on the same computer.

The fourth button from the left on the Language bar is the Handwriting button. The **Handwriting button** displays the **Handwriting menu** (Figure B-2e), which lets you choose the Writing Pad (Figure B-2f), Write Anywhere (Figure B-2g), or the on-screen keyboard (Figure B-2h). The **On-Screen Symbol Keyboard command** on the Handwriting menu displays an on-screen keyboard that allows you to enter special symbols that are not available on a standard keyboard. You can choose only one form of handwriting at a time.

The fifth button indicates which one of the handwriting forms is active. For example, in Figure B-2a the Writing Pad is active. The handwriting recognition capabilities of text services will be discussed shortly.

The sixth button from the left on the Language bar is the Help button. The **Help button** displays the Help menu. If you click the Language Bar Help command on the Help menu, the Language Bar Help window displays (Figure B-2i). On the far right of the Language bar are two buttons stacked above and below each other. The top button is the Minimize button and the bottom button is the Options button. The **Minimize button** minimizes (hides) the Language bar so that the Language Indicator button displays in the tray status area on the Windows taskbar. The next section discusses the Options button.

Customizing the Language Bar

The down arrow icon immediately below the Minimize button in Figure B-2a is called the Options button. The **Options button** displays a menu of text services options (Figure B-2j). You can use this menu to hide the Speech Tools, Handwriting, and Help buttons on the Language bar by clicking their names to remove the check mark to the left of each button. The Settings command on the Options menu displays a dialog box that lets you customize the Language bar. This command will be discussed shortly. The Restore Defaults command redisplays hidden buttons on the Language bar.

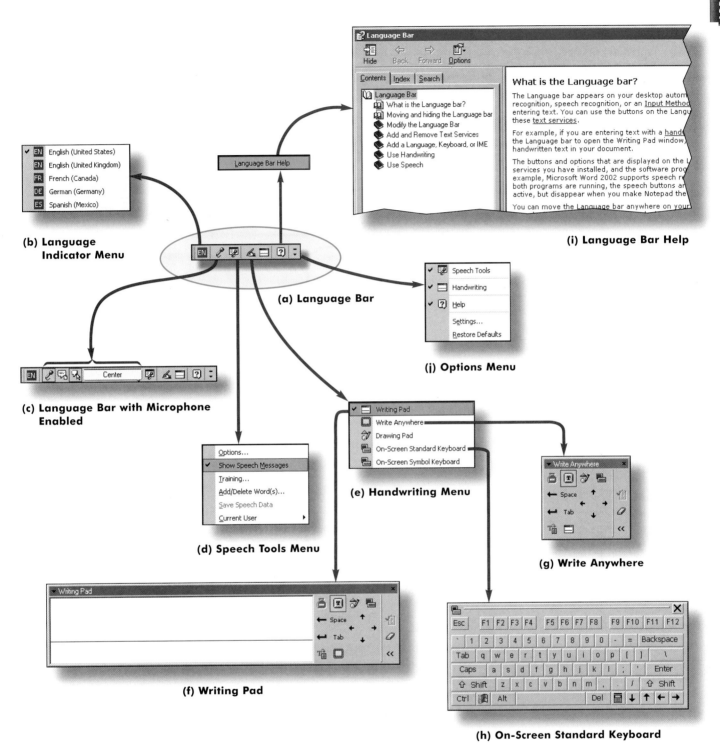

FIGURE B-2

If you right-click the Language bar, a shortcut menu displays (Figure B-3a on the next page). This shortcut menu lets you further customize the Language bar. The **Minimize command** on the shortcut menu minimizes the Language bar the same as the Minimize button on the Language bar. The **Transparency command** toggles the Language bar between being solid and transparent. You can see through a transparent Language bar (Figure B-3b). The **Text Labels command** toggles text labels on the Language bar on (Figure B-3c) and off (Figure B-3a). The **Additional icons in taskbar command** toggles between only showing the Language Indicator button in the tray status area and showing icons that represent the text services that are active (Figure B-3d).

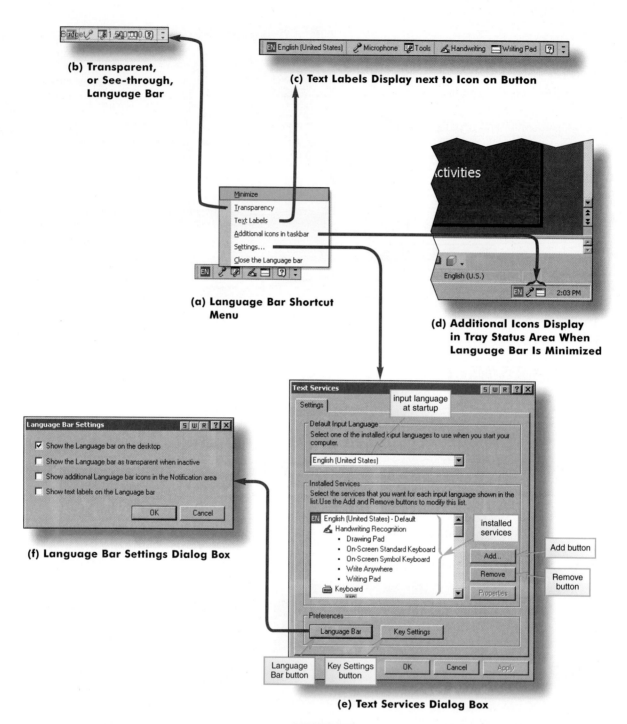

FIGURE B-3

The **Settings command** displays the Text Services dialog box (Figure B-3e). The **Text Services dialog box** allows you to select the language at startup; add and remove text services; modify keys on the keyboard; and modify the Language bar. If you want to remove any one of the entries in the Installed Services list, select the entry, and then click the Remove button. If you want to add a service, click the Add button. The Key Settings button allows you to modify the keyboard. If you click the **Language Bar button** in the Text Services dialog box, the **Language Bar Settings dialog box** displays (Figure B-3f). This dialog box contains Language bar options, some of which are the same as the commands on the Language bar shortcut menu described earlier.

The **Close the Language bar command** on the shortcut menu shown in Figure B-3a closes the Language bar and hides the Language Indicator button in the tray status area on the Windows taskbar. If you close the Language bar and want to redisplay it, follow the instructions at the top of page PP B.02.

Speech Recognition

The **Speech Recognition service** available with Office XP enables your computer to recognize human speech through a microphone. The microphone has two modes: dictation and voice command (Figure B-4). You switch between the two modes by clicking the Dictation button and the Voice Command button on the Language bar. These buttons display only when you turn on Speech Recognition by clicking the **Microphone button** on the Language bar (Figure B-5 on the next page). If you are using the Microphone button for the very first time in PowerPoint, it will require that you check your microphone settings and step through voice training before activating the Speech Recognition service.

The **Dictation button** places the microphone in Dictation mode. In **Dictation mode**, whatever you speak is entered as text in the active cell. The **Voice Command button** places the microphone in Voice Command mode. In **Voice Command mode**, whatever you speak is interpreted as a command. If you want to turn off the microphone, click the Microphone button on the Language bar or in Voice Command mode say, "Mic off" (pronounced mike off). It is important to remember that minimizing the Language bar does not turn off the microphone.

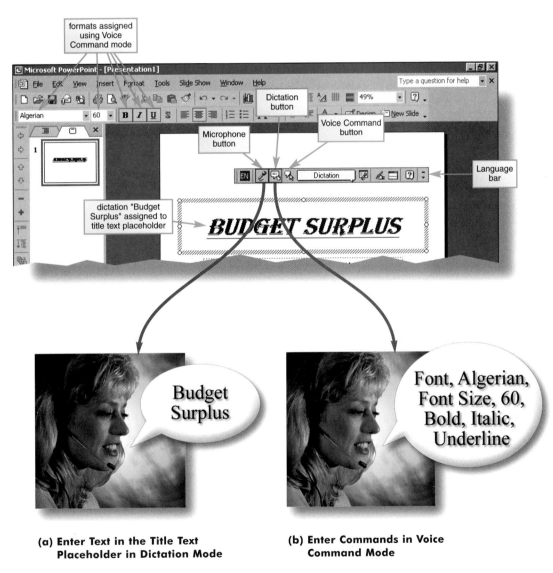

(a) Enter Text in the Title Text
Placeholder in Dictation Mode

(b) Enter Commands in Voice
Command Mode

FIGURE B-4

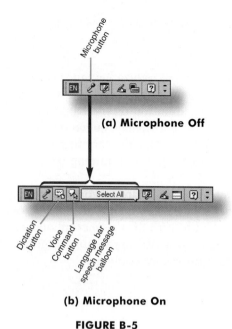

(a) Microphone Off

(b) Microphone On

FIGURE B-5

The **Language bar speech message balloon** shown in Figure B-5b displays messages that may offer help or hints. In Voice Command mode, the name of the last recognized command you said displays. If you use the mouse or keyboard instead of the microphone, a message will appear in the Language bar speech message balloon indicating the word you could say. In Dictation mode, the message, Dictating, usually displays. The Speech Recognition service, however, will display messages to inform you that you are talking too soft, too loud, too fast, or to ask you to repeat what you said by displaying, What was that?

Getting Started with Speech Recognition

For the microphone to function properly, you should follow these steps:

1. Make sure your computer meets the minimum requirements.
2. Install Speech Recognition.
3. Set up and position your microphone, preferably a close-talk headset with gain adjustment support.
4. Train Speech Recognition.

The following sections describe these steps in more detail.

SPEECH RECOGNITION SYSTEM REQUIREMENTS   For Speech Recognition to work on your computer, it needs the following:

1. Microsoft Windows 98 or later or Microsoft Windows NT 4.0 or later
2. At least 128 MB RAM
3. 400 MHz or faster processor
4. Microphone and sound card

INSTALLING SPEECH RECOGNITION   If Speech Recognition is not installed on your computer, start Microsoft Word and then click Speech on the Tools menu.

SETUP AND POSITION YOUR MICROPHONE   Set up your microphone as follows:

1. Connect your microphone to the sound card in the back of the computer.
2. Position the microphone approximately one inch out from and to the side of your mouth. Position it so you are not breathing into it.
3. On the Language bar, click the Speech Tools button, and then click Options (Figure B-6a).
4. When the Speech Properties dialog box displays (Figure B-6b), if necessary, click the Speech Recognition tab.
5. Click the Configure Microphone button. Follow the Microphone Wizard directions as shown in Figures B-6c, B-6d, and B-6e. The Next button will remain dimmed in Figure B-6d until the volume meter consistently stays in the green area.
6. If someone else installed Speech Recognition, click the New button in the Speech Properties dialog box and enter your name. Click the Train Profile button and step through the Voice Training Wizard. The Voice Training Wizard will require that you enter your gender and age group. It then will step you through voice training.

You can adjust the microphone further by clicking the **Settings button** (Figure B-6b) in the Speech Properties dialog box. The Settings button displays the **Recognition Profile Settings dialog box** that allows you to adjust the pronunciation sensitivity and accuracy versus recognition response time.

(a) **Speech Tools Menu**

(b) **Speech Properties Dialog Box**

(c) **Adjust Microphone**

(d) **Adjust Volume**

(e) **Test Microphone**

FIGURE B-6

TRAIN THE SPEECH RECOGNITION SERVICE   The Speech Recognition service will understand most commands and some dictation without any training at all. It will recognize much more of what you speak, however, if you take the time to train it. After one training session, it will recognize 85 to 90 percent of your words. As you do more training, accuracy will rise to 95 percent. If you feel that too many mistakes are being made, then continue to train the service. The more training you do, the more accurately it will work for you. Follow these steps to train the Speech Recognition service:

(a) Speech Tools Menu

(b) Voice Training Dialog Box

FIGURE B-7

1. Click the Speech Tools button on the Language bar and then click Training (Figure B-7a).
2. When the **Voice Training dialog box** displays (Figure B-7b), click one of the sessions and then click the Next button.
3. Complete the training session, which should take less than 15 minutes.

If you are serious about using a microphone to speak to your computer, you need to take the time to go through at least three of the eight training sessions listed in Figure B-7b.

Using Speech Recognition

Speech recognition lets you enter text into a worksheet similarly to speaking into a tape recorder. Instead of typing, you can dictate text that you want to assign to cells, and you can issue voice commands. In **Voice Command mode**, you can speak menu names, commands on menus, toolbar button names, and dialog box option buttons, check boxes, list boxes, and button names. Speech Recognition, however, is not a completely hands-free form of input. Speech recognition works best if you use a combination of your voice, the keyboard, and the mouse. You soon will discover that Dictation mode is far less accurate than Voice Command mode. Table B-1 lists some tips that will improve the Speech Recognition service's accuracy considerably.

Table B-1	Tips to Improve Speech Recognition
NUMBER	**TIP**
1	The microphone hears everything. Though the Speech Recognition service filters out background noise, it is recommended that you work in a quiet environment.
2	Try not to move the microphone around once it is adjusted.
3	Speak in a steady tone and speak clearly.
4	In Dictation mode, do not pause between words. A phrase is easier to interpret than a word. Sounding out syllables in a word will make it more difficult for the Speech Recognition service to interpret what you are saying.
5	If you speak too loudly or too softly, it makes it difficult for the Speech Recognition service to interpret what you said. Check the Language bar speech message balloon for an indication that you may be speaking too loudly or too softly.
6	If you experience problems after training, adjust the recognition options that control accuracy and rejection by clicking the Settings button shown in Figure B-6b on the previous page.
7	When you are finished using the microphone, turn it off by clicking the Microphone button on the Language bar or in Voice Command mode say, "Mic off." Leaving the microphone on is the same as leaning on the keyboard.
8	If the Speech Recognition service is having difficulty with unusual words, then add the words to its dictionary by using the Add/Delete Word(s) command on the Speech Tools menu (Figure B-8a). The last names of individuals and the names of companies are good examples of the types of words you should add to the dictionary.
9	Training will improve accuracy; practice will improve confidence.

The last command on the Speech Tools menu is the Current User command (Figure B-8a). The **Current User command** is useful for multiple users who share a computer. It allows them to configure their own individual profiles, and then switch between users as they use the computer.

For additional information on the Speech Recognition service, click the Help button on the Standard toolbar, click the Answer Wizard tab, and search for the phrase, Speech Recognition.

Handwriting Recognition

Using the Office XP handwriting recognition capabilities, you can enter text and numbers into PowerPoint by writing instead of typing. You can write using a special handwriting device that connects to your computer or you can write on the screen using your mouse. Four basic methods of handwriting are available by clicking the **Handwriting button** on the Language bar: Writing Pad; Write Anywhere; On-Screen Standard Keyboard; and On-Screen Symbol Keyboard. Although the on-screen keyboards do not involve handwriting recognition, they are part of the Handwriting menu and, therefore, will be discussed in this section. While the Drawing Pad command displays on the Handwriting menu, it functions only in Microsoft Word and Outlook.

If your Language bar does not include the Handwriting button (Figures B-1b or B-1c on page PP B.01), then for installation instructions click the Help button on the Standard toolbar, click the Answer Wizard tab, and search for the phrase Install Handwriting Recognition.

(a) Speech Tools Menu

(b) Add/Delete Word(s) Dialog Box

FIGURE B-8

Writing Pad

To display the Writing Pad, click the Handwriting button on the Language bar and then click Writing Pad (Figure B-9 on the next page). The **Writing Pad** resembles a note pad with one or more lines on which you can use freehand to print or write in cursive. With the **Text button** enabled, you can form letters on the line by moving the mouse while holding down the mouse button. To the right of the note pad is a rectangular toolbar. Use the buttons on this toolbar to adjust the Writing Pad, select cells, and activate other handwriting applications.

Consider the example in Figure B-9. With the subtitle text placeholder selected, the word, State, is written in cursive on the **Pen line** in the Writing Pad. As soon as the word is complete, the Handwriting Recognition service automatically assigns the word to the subtitle text placeholder.

FIGURE B-9

You can customize the Writing Pad by clicking the **Options button** on the left side of the title bar and then clicking the Options command (Figure B-10a). Invoking the **Options command** causes the Handwriting Options dialog box to display. The **Handwriting Options dialog box** contains two sheets: Common and Writing Pad. The **Common sheet** lets you change the pen color and pen width, adjust recognition, and customize the toolbar area of the Writing Pad. The **Writing Pad sheet** allows you to change the background color and the number of lines that display in the Writing Pad. Both sheets contain a **Restore Default button** to restore the settings to what they were when the software was installed initially.

When you first start using the Writing Pad, you may want to remove the check mark from the **Automatic recognition check box** on the Common sheet in the Handwriting Options dialog box (Figure B-10b). With the check mark removed, the Handwriting Recognition service will not interpret what you write in the Writing Pad until you click the **Recognize Now button** on the toolbar (Figure B-9). This allows you to pause and adjust your writing.

The best way to learn how to use the Writing Pad is to practice with it. Also, for more information, click the Help button on the Standard toolbar, click the Answer Wizard tab, and search for the phrase, Handwriting Recognition.

(a) Writing Pad Options Menu

(b) Handwriting Options Dialog Box
with Common Sheet Active

(c) Handwriting Options Dialog Box
with Writing Pad Sheet Active

FIGURE B-10

Write Anywhere

Rather than use a Writing Pad, you can write anywhere on the screen by invoking the **Write Anywhere command** on the Handwriting menu (Figure B-11 on the next page) that displays when you click the Handwriting button on the Language bar. In this case, the entire window is your writing pad.

In Figure B-11, the word, By, is written in cursive using the mouse button. Shortly after you finish writing the word, the Handwriting Recognition service interprets it, assigns it to the subtitle text placeholder, and erases what you wrote.

It is recommended that when you first start using the Writing Anywhere service that you remove the check mark from the Automatic recognition check box in the Common sheet in the Handwriting Options dialog box (Figure B-10b). With the check mark removed, the Handwriting Recognition service will not interpret what you write on the screen until you click the Recognize Now button on the toolbar (Figure B-11).

FIGURE B-11

On-Screen Standard Keyboard

The **On-Screen Standard Keyboard command** on the Handwriting menu (Figure B-12) displays an on-screen keyboard. An **on-screen keyboard** lets you enter data into a cell by using your mouse to click the keys. The on-screen keyboard is similar to the type found on handheld computers.

FIGURE B-12

On-Screen Symbol Keyboard

The **On-Screen Symbol Keyboard** command on the Handwriting menu displays a special on-screen keyboard that allows you to enter symbols that are not on your keyboard. To display this keyboard, click the Handwriting button on the Language bar and then click On-Screen Symbol Keyboard (Figure B-13). Clicking the Shift key displays capital letters.

Some symbols are letters in various languages, such as the Latin Þ (thorn), Greek β (beta) and the Latin letter o with slash (Ø). A few of these symbols also are used in mathematical and scientific applications. For example, Ø represents the null set in mathematics when a set has no elements. It also is used to indicate a zero reading when current or voltage is measured on a scale.

The **diacritic symbols** on the keyboard are marks, points, or signs printed above or below a letter to indicate its exact pronunciation or accent. For example, the acute accent on the letter e (é) is used in French words such as attaché and cliché. The cedilla (ç) and circumflex accent (^) are used in the French translation for the phrase, the more that changes, the more it is the same thing: plus ça change, plus c'est la même chose, shown in Figure B-13.

The **ligature symbols** on the keyboard are characters consisting of two or more letters joined together. The Latin small ligature œ, for example, is used in the French word cœur, meaning heart.

Three currency abbreviations also are located on the On-Screen Symbol Keyboard. They include the Euro (€), the British pound (£), and the Japanese yen (¥).

Table B-2 lists some of the symbols on the On-Screen Symbol Keyboard and their uses.

FIGURE B-13

Table B-2 On-Screen Symbol Keyboard Keys

KEY	NAME	EXAMPLE
Currency		
€	Euro sign	€875
£	Pound sign	£250
¥	Yen sign	¥500
Mathematics and Science		
β	Beta	$\beta = \omega * c / \lambda$
Ø	Empty (null) set	$A \cap B = \emptyset$
/	Fraction slash	4/2
μ	Micro sign (mu)	μ-inches
δ	Partial differential (delta)	$\delta y/\delta x$
±	Plus-minus sign	12 ± 2 inches
Diacritic		
´	Acute accent	Attaché, cliché
ç	Cedilla	Façade
^	Circumflex accent	Même
à	Grave accent	À la mode
~	Tilde	Niño
ü	Umlaut	Naïve
Ligature		
æ	Latin small ligature æ	Encyclopædia Britannica
œ	Latin small ligature œ	Cœur
Miscellaneous		
¿	Inverted question mark	¿Qué pasa?
§	Section	15 U.S. Code §1601

APPENDIX C
Publishing Office Web Pages to a Web Server

With the Office applications, you use the Save as Web Page command on the File menu to save the Web page to a Web server using one of two techniques: Web folders or File Transfer Protocol. A **Web folder** is an Office shortcut to a Web server. **File Transfer Protocol** (**FTP**) is an Internet standard that allows computers to exchange files with other computers on the Internet.

You should contact your network system administrator or technical support staff at your ISP to determine if their Web server supports Web folders, FTP, or both, and to obtain necessary permissions to access the Web server. If you decide to publish Web pages using a Web folder, you must have the Office Server Extensions (OSE) installed on your computer.

Using Web Folders to Publish Office Web Pages

When publishing to a Web folder, someone first must create the Web folder before you can save to it. If you are granted permission to create a Web folder, you must obtain the URL of the Web server, a user name, and possibly a password that allows you to access the Web server. You also must decide on a name for the Web folder. Table C-1 explains how to create a Web folder.

Office adds the name of the Web folder to the list of current Web folders. You can save to this folder, open files in the folder, rename the folder, or perform any operations you would to a folder on your hard disk. You can use your Office program or Windows Explorer to access this folder. Table C-2 explains how to save to a Web folder.

Using FTP to Publish Office Web Pages

When publishing a Web page using FTP, you first must add the FTP location to your computer before you can save to it. An **FTP location**, also called an **FTP site**, is a collection of files that reside on an FTP server. In this case, the FTP server is the Web server.

To add an FTP location, you must obtain the name of the FTP site, which usually is the address (URL) of the FTP server, and a user name and a password that allows you to access the FTP server. You save and open the Web pages on the FTP server using the name of the FTP site. Table C-3 explains how to add an FTP site.

Office adds the name of the FTP site to the FTP locations list in the Save As and Open dialog boxes. You can open and save files using this list. Table C-4 explains how to save to an FTP location.

Table C-1 Creating a Web Folder

1. Click File on the menu bar and then click Save As (or Open).
2. When the Save As dialog box (or Open dialog box) displays, click My Network Places (or Web Folders) on the Places Bar. Double-click Add Network Place (or Add Web Folder).
3. When the Add Network Place Wizard dialog box displays, click the Create a new Network Place option button and then click the Next button. Type the URL of the Web server in the Folder location text box, enter the folder name you want to call the Web folder in the Folder name text box, and then click the Next button. Click Empty Web and then click the Finish button.
4. When the Enter Network Password dialog box displays, type the user name and, if necessary, the password in the respective text boxes and then click the OK button.
5. Close the Save As or the Open dialog box.

Table C-2 Saving to a Web Folder

1. Click File on the menu bar and then click Save As.
2. When the Save As dialog box displays, type the Web page file name in the File name text box. Do not press the ENTER key.
3. Click My Network Places on the Places Bar.
4. Double-click the Web folder name in the Save in list.
5. If the Enter Network Password dialog box displays, type the user name and password in the respective text boxes and then click the OK button.
6. Click the Save button in the Save As dialog box.

Table C-3 Adding an FTP Location

1. Click File on the menu bar and then click Save As (or Open).
2. In the Save As dialog box, click the Save in box arrow and then click Add/Modify FTP Locations in the Save in list; or in the Open dialog box, click the Look in box arrow and then click Add/Modify FTP Locations in the Look in list.
3. When the Add/Modify FTP Locations dialog box displays, type the name of the FTP site in the Name of FTP site text box. If the site allows anonymous logon, click Anonymous in the Log on as area; if you have a user name for the site, click User in the Log on as area and then enter the user name. Enter the password in the Password text box. Click the OK button.
4. Close the Save As or the Open dialog box.

Table C-4 Saving to an FTP Location

1. Click File on the menu bar and then click Save As.
2. When the Save As dialog box displays, type the Web page file name in the File name text box. Do not press the ENTER key.
3. Click the Save in box arrow and then click FTP Locations.
4. Double-click the name of the FTP site to which you wish to save.
5. When the FTP Log On dialog box displays, enter your user name and password and then click the OK button.
6. Click the Save button in the Save As dialog box.

APPENDIX D

Resetting the PowerPoint Toolbars and Menus

PowerPoint customization capabilities allow you to create custom toolbars by adding and deleting buttons and to personalize menus based on their usage. Each time you start PowerPoint, the toolbars and menus display using the same settings as the last time you used it. This appendix shows you how to reset the Standard and Formatting toolbars and menus to their installation settings.

Steps **To Reset the Standard and Formatting Toolbars**

1 **Click the Toolbar Options button on the Standard toolbar and then point to Add or Remove Buttons on the Toolbar Options menu.**

The Toolbar Options menu and the Add or Remove Buttons submenu display (Figure D-1).

FIGURE D-1

2 **Point to Standard on the Add or Remove Buttons submenu. When the Standard submenu displays, scroll down and then point to Reset Toolbar.**

The Standard submenu displays indicating the buttons and boxes that display on the toolbar (Figure D-2). Clicking a button name with a check mark to the left of the name removes the check mark and then removes the button from the toolbar.

3 **Click Reset Toolbar.**

PowerPoint resets the Standard toolbar to its installation settings.

4 **Reset the Formatting toolbar by following Steps 1 through 3 and replacing any reference to the Standard toolbar with the Formatting toolbar.**

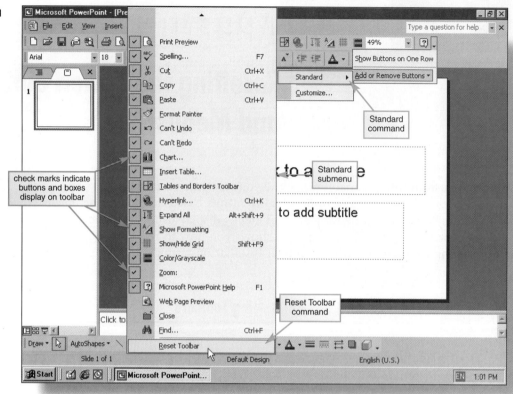

FIGURE D-2

Steps **To Reset Menus**

1 **Click the Toolbar Options button on the Standard toolbar and then point to Add or Remove Buttons on the Toolbar Options menu. Point to Customize on the Add or Remove Buttons submenu.**

The Toolbar Options menu and the Add or Remove Buttons submenu display (Figure D-3).

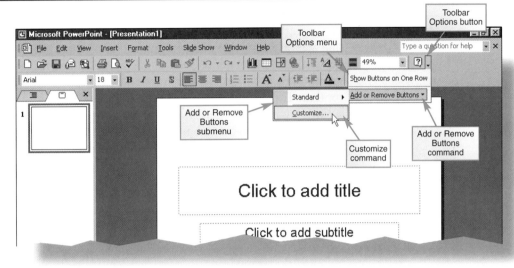

FIGURE D-3

2 **Click Customize. When the Customize dialog box displays, click the Options tab and then point to the Reset my usage data button.**

*The Customize dialog box displays (Figure D-4). The **Customize dialog box** contains three tabbed sheets used for customizing the PowerPoint toolbars and menus.*

3 **Click the Reset my usage data button. When the Microsoft PowerPoint dialog box displays, click the Yes button. Click the Close button in the Customize dialog box.**

PowerPoint resets the menus to the installation settings.

FIGURE D-4

Other **Ways**

1. On View menu point to Toolbars, click Customize on Toolbars submenu, click Options tab, click Reset my usage data button, click Yes button, click Close button

In the **Options sheet** in the Customize dialog box shown in Figure D-4 on the previous page, you can turn off toolbars displaying on two rows and turn off short menus by removing the check marks from the two top check boxes. Click the **Help button** in the lower-left corner of the Customize dialog box to display Help topics that will assist you in customizing toolbars and menus.

Using the **Commands sheet**, you can add buttons to toolbars and commands to menus. Recall that the menu bar at the top of the PowerPoint window is a special toolbar. To add buttons, click the Commands tab in the Customize dialog box. Click a category name in the Categories list and then drag the command name in the Commands list to a toolbar. To add commands to a menu, click a category name in the Categories list, drag the command name in the Commands list to the menu name on the menu bar, and then, when the menu displays, drag the command to the desired location in the menu list of commands.

In the **Toolbars sheet**, you can add new toolbars and reset existing toolbars. If you add commands to menus as described in the previous paragraph and want to reset the menus to their default settings, do the following: (1) Click View on the menu bar and then point to Toolbars; (2) click Customize on the Toolbars submenu; (3) click the Toolbars tab; (4) click Menu Bar in the Toolbars list; (5) click the Reset button; (6) click the OK button; and then (7) click the Close button.

APPENDIX E

Microsoft Office User Specialist Certification Program

What Is MOUS Certification?

The Microsoft Office User Specialist (MOUS) Certification Program provides a framework for measuring your proficiency with the Microsoft Office XP applications, such as Word 2002, Excel 2002, Access 2002, PowerPoint 2002, Outlook 2002, and FrontPage 2002. The levels of certification are described in Table E-1.

Table E-1   Levels of MOUS Certification

LEVEL	DESCRIPTION	REQUIREMENTS	CREDENTIAL AWARDED
Expert	Indicates that you have a comprehensive understanding of the advanced features in a specific Microsoft Office XP application	Pass any ONE of the Expert exams: Microsoft Word 2002 Expert Microsoft Excel 2002 Expert Microsoft Access 2002 Expert Microsoft Outlook 2002 Expert Microsoft FrontPage 2002 Expert	Candidates will be awarded one certificate for each of the Expert exams they have passed: Microsoft Office User Specialist: Microsoft Word 2002 Expert Microsoft Office User Specialist: Microsoft Excel 2002 Expert Microsoft Office User Specialist: Microsoft Access 2002 Expert Microsoft Office User Specialist: Microsoft Outlook 2002 Expert Microsoft Office User Specialist: Microsoft FrontPage 2002 Expert
Core	Indicates that you have a comprehensive understanding of the core features in a specific Microsoft Office 2002 application	Pass any ONE of the Core exams: Microsoft Word 2002 Core Microsoft Excel 2002 Core Microsoft Access 2002 Core Microsoft Outlook 2002 Core Microsoft FrontPage 2002 Core	Candidates will be awarded one certificate for each of the Core exams they have passed: Microsoft Office User Specialist: Microsoft Word 2002 Microsoft Office User Specialist: Microsoft Excel 2002 Microsoft Office User Specialist: Microsoft Access 2002 Microsoft Office User Specialist: Microsoft Outlook 2002 Microsoft Office User Specialist: Microsoft FrontPage 2002
Comprehensive	Indicates that you have a comprehensive understanding of the features in Microsoft PowerPoint 2002	Pass the Microsoft PowerPoint 2002 Comprehensive Exam	Candidates will be awarded one certificate for the Microsoft PowerPoint 2002 Comprehensive exam passed.

Why Should You Get Certified?

Being a Microsoft Office User Specialist provides a valuable industry credential — proof that you have the Office XP applications skills required by employers. By passing one or more MOUS certification exams, you demonstrate your proficiency in a given Office XP application to employers. With over 100 million copies of Office in use around the world, Microsoft is targeting Office XP certification to a wide variety of companies. These companies include temporary employment agencies that want to prove the expertise of their workers, large corporations looking for a way to measure the skill set of employees, and training companies and educational institutions seeking Microsoft Office XP teachers with appropriate credentials.

The MOUS Exams

You pay $50 to $100 each time you take an exam, whether you pass or fail. The fee varies among testing centers. The Expert exams, which you can take up to 60 minutes to complete, consists of between 40 and 60 tasks that you perform online. The tasks require you to use the application just as you would in doing your job. The Core exams contain fewer tasks, and you will have slightly less time to complete them. The tasks you will perform differ on the two types of exams.

How Can You Prepare for the MOUS Exams?

The Shelly Cashman Series® offers several Microsoft-approved textbooks that cover the required objectives on the MOUS exams. For a listing of the textbooks, visit the Shelly Cashman Series MOUS site at scsite.com/offxp/cert.htm and click the link Shelly Cashman Series Office XP Microsoft-Approved MOUS Textbooks (Figure E-1). After using any of the books listed in an instructor-led course, you will be prepared to take the MOUS exam indicated.

How to Find an Authorized Testing Center

You can locate a testing center by calling 1-800-933-4493 in North America or visiting the Shelly Cashman Series MOUS site at scsite.com/offxp/cert.htm and then clicking the link Locate an Authorized Testing Center Near You (Figure E-1). At this Web site, you can look for testing centers around the world.

Shelly Cashman Series MOUS Web Page

The Shelly Cashman Series MOUS Web page (Figure E-1) has more than fifteen Web sites you can visit to obtain additional information on the MOUS Certification Program. The Web page (scsite.com/offxp/cert.htm) includes links to general information on certification, choosing an application for certification, preparing for the certification exam, and taking and passing the certification exam.

FIGURE E-1

Index

Microsoft
POWERPOINT 2002
Quick Reference Summary

In Microsoft PowerPoint 2002, you can accomplish a task in a number of ways. The following table provides a quick reference to each task presented in this textbook. The first column identifies the task. The second column indicates the page number on which the task is discussed in the book. The subsequent four columns list the different ways the task in column one can be carried out. You can invoke the commands listed in the MOUSE, MENU BAR, and SHORTCUT MENU columns using Voice commands.

Microsoft PowerPoint 2002 Quick Reference Summary

TASK	PAGE NUMBER	MOUSE	MENU BAR	SHORTCUT MENU	KEYBOARD SHORTCUT
Animate Text	PP 2.40		Slide Show | Custom Animation | Add Effect button		ALT+D | M
Check Spelling	PP 1.56	Spelling button on Standard toolbar	Tools | Spelling		F7
Clip Art, Add Animation Effects	PP 2.42		Slide Show | Custom Animation		ALT+D | M
Clip Art, Change Size	PP 2.34	Format Picture button on Picture toolbar | Size tab	Format | Picture | Size tab	Format Picture | Size tab	ALT+O | I | Size tab
Clip Art, Insert	PP 2.25	Insert Clip Art button on Drawing toolbar	Insert | Picture | Clip Art		ALT+I | P | C
Clip Art, Move	PP 2.33	Drag			
Delete Text	PP 1.58	Cut button on Standard toolbar	Edit | Cut	Cut	CTRL+X or BACKSPACE or DELETE
Demote a Paragraph on Outline tab	PP 2.13	Demote button on Outlining toolbar			TAB or ALT+SHIFT+RIGHT ARROW
Design Template	PP 1.19	Slide Design button on Formatting toolbar	Format | Slide Design	Slide Design	ALT+O | D
Display a Presentation in Black and White	PP 1.58	Color/Grayscale button on Standard toolbar	View | Color/Grayscale | Pure Black and White		ALT+V | C | U
Edit Web Page through Browser	PPW 1.09	Edit button on Internet Explorer Standard Buttons toolbar	File on browser menu bar | Edit with Microsoft PowerPoint in browser window		ALT+F | D in browser window
E-Mail from PowerPoint	PP 2.52	E-mail button on Standard toolbar	File | Send To | Mail Recipient		ALT+F | D | A
Font	PP 1.25	Font box arrow on Formatting toolbar	Format | Font	Font	ALT+O | F
Font Color	PP 1.25	Font Color button arrow on Formatting toolbar, desired color	Format | Font	Font | Color	ALT+O | F | ALT+C | DOWN ARROW
Font Size, Decrease	PP 1.25	Decrease Font Size button on Formatting toolbar	Format | Font	Font | Size	CTRL+SHIFT+LEFT CARET (<)
Font Size, Increase	PP 1.27	Increase Font Size button on Formatting toolbar	Format | Font	Font | Size	CTRL+SHIFT+RIGHT CARET (>)

Microsoft PowerPoint 2002 Quick Reference Summary *(continued)*

TASK	PAGE NUMBER	MOUSE	MENU BAR	SHORTCUT MENU	KEYBOARD SHORTCUT
Header and Footer, Add to Outline Page	PP 2.37		View | Header and Footer | Notes and Handouts tab		ALT+V | H | Notes and Handouts tab
Help	PP 1.62 and Appendix A	Microsoft PowerPoint Help button on Standard toolbar	Help | Microsoft PowerPoint Help		F1
Italicize	PP 1.26	Italic button on Formatting toolbar	Format | Font | Font style	Font | Font style	CTRL+I
Language Bar	PP 1.18	Language Indicator button in tray	Tools | Speech | Speech Recognition		ALT+T | H | H
Move a Paragraph Down	PP 2.09	Move Down button on Outlining toolbar			ALT+SHIFT+DOWN ARROW
Move a Paragraph Up	PP 2.09	Move Up button on Outlining toolbar			ALT+SHIFT+UP ARROW
New Slide	PP 1.32	New Slide button on Formatting toolbar	Insert | New Slide		CTRL+M
Next Slide	PP 1.46	Next Slide button on vertical scroll bar			PAGE DOWN
Normal View	PP 2.19	Normal View button at lower-left PowerPoint window	View | Normal		ALT+V | N
Open Presentation	PP 1.53	Open button on Standard toolbar	File | Open		CTRL+O
Paragraph Indent, Decrease	PP 1.40	Decrease Indent button on Formatting toolbar			SHIFT+TAB or ALT+SHIFT+ LEFT ARROW
Paragraph Indent, Increase	PP 1.34	Increase Indent button on Formatting toolbar			TAB or ALT+SHIFT+RIGHT ARROW
Previous Slide	PP 1.46	Previous Slide button on vertical scroll bar			PAGE UP
Print a Presentation	PP 1.61	Print button on Standard toolbar	File | Print		CTRL+P
Print Outline	PP 2.48		File | Print | Print what box arrow | Outline View		CTRL+P | TAB | TAB | DOWN ARROW | Outline View
Promote a Paragraph on Outline tab	PP 2.14	Promote button on Outlining toolbar			SHIFT+TAB or ALT+SHIFT+LEFT ARROW
Quit PowerPoint	PP 1.52	Close button on title bar or double-click control icon on title bar	File | Exit		ALT+F4 or CTRL+Q
Redo Action	PP 1.23	Redo button on Standard toolbar	Edit | Redo		CTRL+Y or ALT+E | R
Save a Presentation	PP 1.29	Save button on Standard toolbar	File | Save		CTRL+S
Save as Web Page	PPW 1.03		File | Save as Web Page		ALT+F | G
Slide Layout	PP 2.22		Format | Slide Layout	Slide Layout	ALT+O | L
Slide Show View	PP 1.48	Slide Show button at lower-left PowerPoint window	View | Slide Show		F5 or ALT+V | W
Slide Sorter View	PP 2.18	Slide Sorter View button at lower-left PowerPoint window	View | Slide Sorter		ALT+V | D

Microsoft PowerPoint 2002 Quick Reference Summary

TASK	PAGE NUMBER	MOUSE	MENU BAR	SHORTCUT MENU	KEYBOARD SHORTCUT
Task Pane	PP 1.11		View | Task Pane		ALT+V | K
Toolbar, Reset	Appendix D	Toolbar Options button on toolbar, Add or Remove Buttons, Customize, Toolbars tab		Customize | Toolbars tab	ALT+V | T | C | B
Toolbar, Show Entire	PP 1.12	Double-click move handle			
Undo Action	PP 1.23	Undo button on Standard toolbar	Edit | Undo		CTRL+Z or ALT+E | U
Zoom Percentage, Increase	PP 1.45	Zoom Box arrow on Standard toolbar	View | Zoom		ALT+V | Z